Cross-Country Skiing in the Sierra Nevada

Cross-Country Skiing in the
Sierra Nevada

The Best Resorts & Touring Centers in California & Nevada

Tim Hauserman

The Countryman Press

Woodstock, Vermont

Cross-country skiing is inherently dangerous. Information provided in this book should not substitute for making your own decisions about where and when to ski or how to conduct yourself. You should decide for yourself whether you are capable of skiing on any of the trails mentioned, and take responsibility for being prepared. Be sure to wear and bring proper clothing, water, and food. Tell your friends where you are going and when you should be back. Before embarking on a ski trip check in with the lodge for trail conditions and obtain a copy of the latest map. Trails may no longer be in existence, may be in a different place than on a map, or may not be groomed. Take responsibility for your own actions. Use your brain. Make smart decisions. Prepare for the environment you are entering. The author and The Countryman Press are not responsible for your actions. But have fun.

Note: All of the maps in this book have been provided by their respective resorts and are subject to change. With time, access points may change, and trails, signs, and landmarks referred to in this book may be altered. If you find that such changes have occurred on the trails described in this book, please let the author and the publisher know so that corrections may be made in future editions. The author and publisher also welcome other comments and suggestions. Address all correspondence to:

The Countryman Press
P.O. Box 748
Woodstock, VT 05091

ISBN 978-0-88150-740-9

Book design and composition by Hespenheide Design
Cover photograph © John Dittli Photography
Maps included courtesy of their respective resorts
Interior photographs by the author unless otherwise specified

Published by The Countryman Press, P.O. Box 748, Woodstock, Vermont 05091

Distributed by W.W. Norton & Company, Inc., 500 Fifth Avenue, New York, NY 10110

Printed in the United States of America

10 9 8 7 6 5 4 3 2 1

Dedicated to all those who own, manage, or work at cross-country ski areas. They don't do it for the money, but for the love of the sport. Thank you for creating beautiful places for us to ski.

Contents

Why Cross-Country Ski?   1

Types of Cross-Country Skiing   2

A Few Things to Remember   4

When Can You Ski?   4

Safety   4

Clothing   6

Have the Right Equipment   7

Winter Considerations   9

Search and Rescue   9

Ski Etiquette   10

Looking for a Place to Stay or Something to Eat?   10

How to Enjoy Skiing More   12

Take a Lesson   12

Get in Shape   15

Know Your Animals and Plants   15

Bring the Kids   17

Acknowledgements 85

Final Note 86

Why Cross-Country Ski?

Cross-country skiing: Getting a great workout while enjoying a peaceful, beautiful setting. Or, as Paul Peterson from Bear Valley Cross-Country says, "the most fun you can have with your clothes on." Cross-country skiing is like taking a spectacular hike or epic mountain bike ride in the wilderness, except that you can get a day's worth of exercise in just a few hours.

Cross-country skiing is one of the best aerobic exercises, and instead of sweating away in a smelly gym you get your exercise while gliding over the snow, surrounded by blue skies and the smell of pine trees, working every muscle in your body from your shoulders and arms to your legs and core. Perhaps I am biased, but I believe it is not only the best workout, but also the most fun sport on earth. Not ready for a major aerobic workout, but looking for something to do in winter? Cross-country skiing can accommodate you as well. Shuffle your way slowly across a beautiful, snow-covered meadow, bring your lunch, sit on a rock, and enjoy the day.

The amazing thing is that even on a busy weekend groomed cross-country ski areas attract only a small fraction of the number of skiers found at downhill areas. Once you've made it a few kilometers away from the lodge, you can often ski for hours and only encounter a few other skiers. And those few are usually a great group of people who share your goals: to enjoy exercising in peace and quiet. There is nothing quite like the quiet of cross-country skiing. After a fresh new blanket of snow has fallen and the wind has settled down, it is as quiet as can be. Surrounded by utter stillness, you hear the scrunch of your skis on the snow, perhaps the soft gurgle of a stream nearby, and a few hearty birds.

This will not be news to you, but we live in an overweight, out-of-shape society with an unacceptable percentage of obese people. If you would like to confirm this reality, spend some time at an amusement park or inside any airport or casino in America. There is lengthy debate on the causes of the obesity epidemic, but it seems to me the cause is utterly simple: Americans eat too much and exercise too little. To combat this problem, hundreds of diet programs have been foisted on the populace. Unfortunately, these diets primarily focus on the amount and type of food eaten, with only lip service paid to exercise. To me, we are looking at it backwards. People should be reminded again and again to eat appropriately, but the primary focus should be on burning calories through exercise and taking care of their bodies. Regardless of the diet a person is on, if he sits on his butt at work and then sits on his butt at home, his butt is going to get bigger. It is a pretty simple math equation. To lose weight you need to take in fewer calories then you burn up. To maintain weight, the amount taken in and burned up should be about equal. Living a sedentary lifestyle doesn't burn up very many calories, so in order to lose weight a person has to starve himself on a miniscule diet of just a few boring calories. If you are cross-country skiing regularly all winter, however, you can afford to eat delicious food and be healthy at the same time—a great concept for anyone.

Cross-country skiing has everything needed to escape spare-tire land: Wonderful outdoor aerobic exercise that burns a lot of calories while offering a chance to commune with nature, peace and quiet, and a low-key, relaxed atmosphere away from the hustle, bustle, and big money of downhill ski resorts. If everyone in America who lived close to a cross-country ski area would hit the trails a few times a week, a big chunk of fat would be removed from our collective beer bellies.

There are a million different reasons to cross-country ski. The best thing to do is to clip into your skis, find a great resort nearby and get out there!

Types of Cross-Country Skiing

Cross-country skiing is divided into a number of different disciplines; I've done my best to summarize them in the paragraphs that follow. The primary focus of this book is skiing at the renowned groomed nordic centers in the Sierra Nevada. Touring will be touched on, but downhill backcountry skiing will have to wait for its own book.

Cross-country touring Cross-country tourers go out into the woods to ski through meadows and up and down gentle hills. Tourers sometimes ski in fresh pow-

Another beautiful day cross-country skiing at Kirkwood

der, but often ski in the tracks created by other skiers. When ski touring, skiers usually stride in the flats or gentle hills, then herringbone or sidestep if it gets too steep. *Striding* means skiing with a walking motion. The skis point straight ahead and glide forward and back with each motion. Touring or striding skis come in narrower, nonmetal-edged varieties as well as wider, metal-edged varieties designed for going down steeper hills. For many people, touring is what they envision when they think of cross-country skiing. You park your car at the end of the road, put on your skis, and slide away.

Nordic center striding At groomed nordic ski centers, a set of tracks is set (along with a skating lane; more about that later). These tracks make it easy to stride, and skiers can get up a good head of steam either with touring gear, or even better, with racing striding gear. Skiing in tracks allows you to ski much more smoothly than when flailing around in the trees, and it is really hard to get lost at a cross-country center. While touring allows you to explore the quiet of nature, striding in set tracks gives you a better opportunity for a steady aerobic workout.

Nordic center skate skiing The skate skiing motion is similar to the motion used when ice skating or in-line skating. Skate skis are shorter, narrower, and lighter than touring gear, and are only effective for skating on groomed or firmly packed surfaces. Skate poles are longer, and skating boots are higher and stiffer than touring boots. For most skiers, skating is quite a bit faster and more aerobic than striding (although those who master the art of striding would beg to differ), and maybe for those reasons has become the most popular form of skiing at cross-country ski centers, especially for intermediate to advanced skiers. Skating for many tends to be harder to learn than striding, and many instructors recommend getting comfortable on your striding skis before advancing to skating.

Backcountry downhill skiing (randonee or telemark) Randonee and telemark skiing involve skinning up steeper slopes for the thrill of skiing back down them. *Skins* are long strips that attach to the bottom of the skis and allow the skier to walk up steeper slopes without sliding backward. At the top, the skins are removed for the ski down. The skis used are similar to downhill skis, but the the heel of the boot is not connected to the ski when hiking up. When randonee skiers reach the top of the mountain they snap their heels into the back of the binding and ski as if at a downhill resort. Telemark skiers leave their heels free. Backcountry skiers are often experienced at downhill skiing, but are sick of the crowds found at downhill resorts. In the backcountry they find a more peaceful, natural setting and get the workout of going up the hill as well as down.

A Few Things to Remember

Before you put on those skis, you need to know a few things . . .

When Can You Ski?

The short answer is when there is enough snow on the ground. Winters in the Sierra Nevada vary a great deal from year to year. In some years it starts snowing hard in October and doesn't seem to slow down until June. The following year you might be lucky to be able to ski by Christmas. "Normal" is only an average, but normally you can cross-country ski from the end of November until mid-April. While most nordic ski areas are anxious to open as soon as there is enough snow, some will close in spring when they could probably hold on for a few more weeks. Springtime closures at some resorts are based more on economics, that is, a lack of skiers, not a lack of snow. Once the temperatures in the Bay Area and the Sacramento Valley reach 70 degrees, the families who live there tend to switch to golf and tennis. Those of us who are addicted to cross-country skiing plead with these folks to put off the summertime activities for a few more weeks. What is the hurry? You will have plenty of time to ride your bike, but when the skiing is over, it is over for at least six months.

Compared to alpine ski resorts, cross-country ski areas are at a bit of a disadvantage when it comes to snow coverage because they are usually located at lower elevations in more open terrain. Many Sierra winter storms, especially those early in the season, will drop snow above 7,000 feet, but rain at lower elevations. Most nordic centers have base lodges in the 6,000- to 6,500-foot range, so they need to wait for the big, cold winter storms to get up and running.

On the other hand, nordic centers can often create great skiing conditions with very little snow. The moral of the story is cross-country skiing is like a good life—short and sweet. As soon as the snow comes, get out there and ski!

Safety

Follow these tips for a safe cross-country ski experience:

- ***Make a plan.*** When heading out to cross-

Point Mariah Hut at Royal Gorge looking towards the Sierra crest

country ski, be sure to tell people where you are going and when you will return. Then stick to the schedule and let your friends know when you have returned.

- *Accurately assess your ability and make sure that you are capable of handling the level of difficulty of your chosen route.* If you are skiing at a nordic center, employees in the lodge can help you interpret the trail map. If, however, you are skiing in an area away from a nordic center, you must do your own research to make sure you are capable of skiing in your selected location. If you are a novice, it is a good idea to ski at a groomed area first, as there are usually a number of trails that are suited to beginners.

- *Drink plenty of water.* People have a tendency to forget that even when it is cold outside, they still need lots of water when they are exercising. And be sure to eat, even if it is just a small snack to keep your energy level up (although it is less likely you'll forget you're hungry!).

- *Avoid hypothermia and frostbite.*

Hypothermia is the reduction of the body's core temperature as a result of exposure to cold and moisture. If a skier gets hypothermia it is usually because her clothes became wet with sweat and then she was exposed to cold and wind. Frostbite is the freezing of body tissues due to prolonged exposure to the cold. Nordic skiers are most likely to get frostbite after they lose their gloves or get their feet wet; the most vulnerable body parts are the toes and fingers. Prevention is the key to avoiding hypothermia and frostbite. Do your best to stay dry and warm, and always wear layers. If you wear athletic clothing that is designed for skiing (clothing that wicks moisture away from your body and dries quickly; see pages 6–7), take prudent precautions, and don't get lost, you should be okay.

- *Be aware if you are skiing in avalanche-prone areas.* In general, cross-country ski areas are situated in locations that are not steep enough to create avalanches. Winter athletes, however, should understand where and why avalanches occur. Avalanches are most likely to occur on relatively steep slopes (very steep slopes do not hold enough snow to avalanche), on the lee side of mountains (you'll see that the snow forms cornices), or in gullies. You are most vulnerable to an avalanche right after or during a storm. The bigger and wetter the storm, the bigger the risk. A level one avalanche course is highly recommended for skiers, snowshoers, or snowmobiliers who spend time in the backcountry.

- *Carry the appropriate food and gear.* Water, snacks, lunch, sunscreen, and additional clothing layers all may be needed. If you are skiing outside of a nordic center or out for a long ski, then you may want to bring a small first-aid kit, compass or GPS receiver, and map. If you are backcountry skiing or in terrain that may avalanche, take a small shovel and avalanche beacon.

- **Protect yourself from the sun.** Even if the temperature is cold, the sun can be quite intense when it reflects off the snow at high altitudes. Always wear sunscreen on your face and other body parts that might be exposed. If you are skiing in your short sleeves on a warm spring day, remember to apply sunscreen to your arms. The snow's reflection also makes it essential to wear sunglasses or goggles.
- **At high elevations, watch for altitude sickness.** While most cross-country ski areas are situated in areas below 9,000 feet, people who live in the "flatlands," may still have issues with the altitude. The most common symptoms of mild altitude sickness are shortness of breath, headache, fatigue, and loss of appetite. So when you are tired after that long, steep climb, blame it on the altitude, not on your conditioning. To avoid any symptoms drink plenty of liquids, and instead of immediately hitting the trail when you arrive in the mountains, try to spend some time getting used to the altitude. If you are going to be skiing for several days, take it easy the first day to give your body the opportunity to acclimatize.
- Before traveling to the Sierra Nevada, review "Winter Considerations" (page 9) and "Search and Rescue" (pages 9–10), and then be sure you are adequately prepared for winter conditions. Be careful out there!

Clothing

When considering what to wear when cross-country skiing it is best to start with three principles:

1. **Wear lightweight synthetic clothing.** Cotton clothing gets wet and very uncomfortable because it soaks up moisture like a sponge. Wearing wet clothes can quickly lead to frostbite and hypothermia.
2. **Use a layering system.** This will allow you to take clothes on and off as the weather and your level of activity dictates. Remember that if you are not wearing a layer, you will be carrying it so it really pays to use only lightweight clothing.

Happy skiing in the trees at Tahoe Cross-Country

3. **You will be warmer than you think.** Nordic skiing is aerobic and you will warm up pretty fast. The clothing that you would wear for downhill skiing is probably much too warm and bulky for cross-country skiing: Instead of spending time on a chairlift getting cold you will be huffing and puffing your way up a hill. The clothing that you would wear on a cold and rainy run or hike would be appropriate for cross-country skiing.

With those three principles in mind, let's look at some specifics:

Lower body Start out with a pair of synthetic-fabric underwear. Then add cross-country ski pants. They come in a variety of styles, but the general premise is that they are slightly loose-fitting athletic tights that repel water and are thick enough to keep you warm, but not so thick that you will get too warm. Check with your outdoor clothing supplier for the latest product. Some skiers prefer to wear long johns with wind pants over the top. If it is snowing or raining hard you can wear a pair of waterproof pants over your cross-country tights, but make sure it is really necessary. As hard as you will be working, if it is not very cold you will bake in waterproof pants.

Upper body On the upper body many skiers feel most comfortable with a lightweight synthetic layer topped with a fleece vest that can be removed as you warm up. Fleece fabrics that you may have heard of include polypropylene and capilene. Some add a lightweight shell over the top of the fleece layer for wind protection, especially for long downhills. If it is snowing, consider a lightweight rain shell. I try to avoid the rainproof pants, but find it is important to keep my upper body warm and dry, and a lightweight shell performs this nicely.

The front of the pack in The Great Ski Race

Head If it is very cold, go for a warm hat, but usually a baseball-style cap is adequate for most people skiing at nordic centers in the Sierra Nevada. The bill provides shelter from the sun and snow, while fleece hats can be too warm and fail to protect your eyes from the elements. Whatever you do, wear some sort of hat, because a tremendous amount of body heat escapes through your head.

Hands Lightweight, water-resistant or waterproof gloves work best. Your hands are working hard, so don't make the mistake of putting on gloves that you would wear downhill skiing, you will be ripping them off your sweaty hands after about 100 yards. Ask your nordic clothing retailer for the best gloves for your skiing plans.

Have the Right Equipment

In some sports, top-of-the-line equipment is only suited for experts, but in nordic skiing the best equipment helps everyone ski better. After you have decided that skiing is for you and you feel comfortable spending the money, you will get a good return on your investment by purchasing the best cross-country ski gear. If you are not ready for the commitment, you can find good skis and equipment that you will enjoy at a reasonable price. If you are just starting out in the sport, keep your eyes open for ski swaps, which usually occur in the fall. Tahoe Cross-Country Ski Area in Tahoe City has a good one every November. Some of the nordic areas also sell used gear at good prices, especially at the end of the ski season.

Gear for Every Skier

Pack Depending upon the length of your trip, you can carry a single-bottle pack, a small two-bottle fanny pack with room for a layer or two of clothes, or a Camelback or other hydration system. While I love my hydration pack for bike riding and hiking, I find it to be a hindrance when cross-country skiing, as it restricts the free movement of my arms. Whatever pack you take, make sure it is small and light, but big enough to carry the basics: Water, snack, extra layer of clothing, car keys, and a small first-aid kit. If you are skiing all day, bring a pack that is big enough to carry lunch.

Gear for Striders

Skis Striding gear comes in a number of different forms and price ranges. If you only want one pair of striding skis and you would like to ski at a nordic center as well as tootle around in the woods, attempt to find a pair that is wide enough to ski through the powder, but narrow enough to be fast in the tracks. If you plan on striding only in the set tracks at a nordic center, you will probably appreciate a lighter, narrower pair that will enable you to ski faster with less effort. These skis, more designed for racing, come in waxless and waxable varieties. The advantages of waxless skis, which have a fish-scale or similar pattern impressed in the skis' kick zone, is that you need only hot-wax the tips and tails of the skis, and that they function over a wide variety of snow conditions. Waxable skis require a more extensive knowledge of waxing in relation to snow surfaces; expect to learn words like *klister* and *universal*. If done properly, waxable skis are faster and smoother than waxless. In addition, waxable skis cruise quietly down the tracks instead of making the obnoxious grating sound of fish scales on snow.

Boots Ski boots for striding come in a variety of styles. Make sure your boots provide adequate ankle support. The type of boot you buy depends upon your budget. If you will be skiing infrequently or plan on concentrating mostly on skate skiing, then it doesn't make sense to spend a ton of money on striding boots. On the other hand, if this is going to be your regular sport, by all means make the investment in high-quality boots. The key, of course, is to get a pair that fit comfortably. Try them on and take a long walk around the shop before purchasing. Many people make the mistake of buying boots that are too tight and pay the price later. There are several different systems of binding-boot combinations; make sure that the binding on your ski matches the type of boot you've selected. If you are a downhill

It snows a lot at Royal Gorge!

skier making the move to cross-country, your feet are going to be very happy—cross-country boots are much more comfortable!

Poles Striding poles should reach from the ground up to your armpits. If you are purchasing all of your equipment at the same time, you can often get a discount by buying the skis, boots, and poles together.

Skating Gear

The best equipment can make a significant difference in your skating ability. It seems like every year there are new and improved models, and if you can afford it, go for top-of-the-line skis, boots, and poles.

Skis Skating skis are shorter, narrower, and lighter than striding skis. Check with your nordic retailer for the best style and brand for you. Each brand is a little different, and one may be better suited to your style of skiing than another. Ski areas frequently hold demo days when you can try out new equipment. If you are looking for new gear, attend a demo day and ski different brands to find the best fit for you.

Boots Skating boots are higher and stiffer than striding boots. It is very important to try them on and if possible go for a ski before you buy. There are a number of different designs, and depending upon the width and shape of your foot one brand may be much more com-

fortable than another. If buying all new gear, pick your boots before your skis, and then mount the correct binding for those boots.

Poles Skating poles have smaller baskets than striding poles and are longer: they should go from the ground to somewhere between your chin and your nose. Arm movement and poling is a big part of skate skiing, so a strong but lightweight pole is a good investment.

Gear styles change rapidly. By the time this book comes out some newfangled ski or binding system will have hit the market. Check with your outdoor retailer for information on the latest and greatest. Or refer to the major cross-country ski equipment manufacturers Web sites (addresses are provided in "Resources and Information").

Winter Considerations

If you are surprised to learn that you may encounter snow on your way to the ski area, you may need to read a few other books before going any further in this one. In order to ski you must have snow. Unfortunately, this snow does not only fall where you are skiing, but also on roads, driveways, and decks. If you are traveling in the mountains in winter (and sometimes even in spring and fall, and once in a while in summer) be prepared for snow. Keep close tabs on the weather forecast via television, radio, or the Internet. Be aware that weather forecasts change frequently during stormy periods, and of course they can also be wrong. Armed with as much knowledge as possible, plan for the worst and hope for the best.

The best step you can take to make your journey to your ski destination safer is to make the drive in an all-wheel-drive or four-wheel-drive vehicle with good snow tires. If you do not have such a car, carry chains and know how to put them on. Actually, it is recommended that even all-wheel-drive vehicles carry chains, but in over 25 years of mountain driving with a succession of all-wheel-drive vehicles while living at 7,000 feet and often skiing in the middle of snowstorms, I have never had to put chains on. It is quite rare to see the major highways require chains on four-wheel-drive vehicles with snow tires—the road is usually closed first. If chains are required, you may want to consider staying home watching movies and resting up for a beautiful ski

the next day. If it is a major winter storm, check with the ski area to make sure they are open; if it is really windy and snowing hard, the ski areas will close.

The biggest mistake that people make when driving a four-wheel-drive vehicle is believing they are invincible. You still have to drive with common sense and realize that driving is different when the roads are slick. Slow down. When it is snowy, give two to three times more distance between you and the car in front of you. Turn and brake slowly and smoothly. In fact, do everything in slow motion. Slamming on the brakes and turning quickly causes accidents in the snow. When possible, use gears instead of brakes. Residents of mountain communities like to complain about city drivers not knowing how to drive in the snow, but many of the cars that slide off the edge of the road in a snowstorm are mountain locals driving too fast in their SUVs.

In addition to your ski gear, patience, and a big smile, bring the following in your car during the winter months or during periods when you may encounter snow:

Emergency flares
Small plastic shovel
Warm blanket
Water (a few extra bottles in the trunk is
    a good idea)
Several great CDs or an MP3 player
Extra clothing
Rain-proof pants (for when you are shoveling
    the car out)
Tire chains
Extra snacks
Cell phone
Whistle
Maps
Matches
Deck of cards (in case the road is closed and
    you are stuck waiting)
Giselle Bundchen or Brad Pitt (depending
    upon gender and choice)

Search and Rescue

While it is pretty hard to get lost at a cross-country ski center, when you are touring by yourself in the woods, it is certainly a possibility. If you are lost, remember the acronym STOP: Stop, Think, Observe, Plan. Try to calm yourself and rationally look at where you are. If the snow is not really coming down hard, you can usually retrace your ski tracks and go back to where you began. If it is snowing, but not too hard, you should be able to take a look at nearby landforms to determine how to get back. If you are truly lost in a blizzard, it is best to set up camp and make your location obvious to rescuers so you can be found once the storm abates. (This is a good place to recall the importance of letting someone know where you are going and when you will be back before you venture out on your skiing adventure.)

Ski Etiquette

When skiing or snowshoeing at a groomed cross-country ski area there are rules of etiquette that are important to keeping the sport fun and safe. Follow these 10 to get along better with your fellow skiers:

1. If you are striding, stay in the tracks as much as possible. Skaters go faster and come around those corners quickly. If there is a skier or two or three standing in the middle of the skating lane when a fast-moving skate skier comes around the corner there could be a collision. As turn about is fair play, skate skiers need to be careful not to skate over the classic tracks.

2. Don't block the trail by skiing several abreast. Keep to the right side of the trail (see "fast-moving skate skiers" above).

3. If you are skiing past someone who is slower than you, make sure he knows you are there, then give him a wide berth as you pass.

4. Don't stare at the ground. Look up once in a while and enjoy the scenery. Observe that skier barreling down the hill straight at you (see "fast-moving skate skiers" above).

5. If you are with a group pulling several pulk sleds, ski single file so other skiers can pass.

6. Pack it in, pack it out. Don't leave anything, anywhere, anytime. The last thing the next person skiing on the trail wants to see is your trash.

7. Don't take off your skis and walk on the trail if the snow is soft. You will leave big divots and mess the trail up for the next skier. Either walk off to the side of the trail or just slow down and take your time.

8. Don't bring your dog unless dogs are allowed. Bring a poop bag and use it (see "packing it out"—yes, that does include dog poop).

9. Skiers going downhill always have the right of way.

10. After a ski area closes in the evening do not ski on the trails. The grooming machines will be out and if you ski on the freshly groomed trails your tracks will freeze into ruts during the night. Not nice.

Looking for a Place to Stay or Something to Eat?

I've listed shopping, dining, or lodging possibilities near each ski area. The largest towns in the region are Truckee, Reno, North Lake Tahoe, Carson City, South Lake Tahoe, and Mammoth.

Truckee This former railroad town 14 miles north of Lake Tahoe has seen lots of growth recently, with much more on its way. In 2006, *Outside* magazine cited Truckee as one of the best resort towns in America. While it is certainly a tourist town, it also has a large resident population and an extensive variety of businesses that can supply anything the cross-country skier will need. Tahoe Donner Cross-Country Ski Area is within the town limits. Royal Gorge Ski Resort and Auburn Ski Club are on top of Donner Summit, about 10 miles away. The bustling ski resort and community of Northstar-at-Tahoe is only 5 miles away. Squaw Valley and the Resort at Squaw Creek's cross-country center are 9 miles away.

Reno With a population of over 200,000 and a major international airport, Reno is the largest city close to the Sierra. It is the place to fly into if you are skiing in the Lake Tahoe–Truckee area. Sierra locals go to Reno to get a Home Depot, Trader Joe's, or REI fix; if you are looking for a quiet mountain community in the pines, Reno is not it. If you are looking for casino gaming, shows, and inexpensive midweek housing, Reno may fit the bill. The cross-country ski resorts of Royal Gorge, Tahoe Donner, Auburn Ski Club, Spooner Lake,

Northstar and Tahoe Cross-Country are all within an hour's drive (weather permitting).

North Lake Tahoe The series of small communities situated on the northern shores of Lake Tahoe are collectively known as North Lake Tahoe. Starting from the southwest and going to the northeast, these include Tahoma/Homewood, Tahoe City, Kings Beach, and Incline Village. There are a number of restaurants, shops, and grocery stores, and best of all, the large and beautiful Lake Tahoe right out the window. Each town has its own flare and style. Homewood and its neighbor Tahoma are located on Tahoe's quieter west shore, which gets massive amounts of snow. They are backed up to Desolation Wilderness, a true gem of the Tahoe region. When the 1960 Winter Olympics were held in nearby Squaw Valley, the cross-country ski events were held where Sugar Pine State Park is now located, just to the south and west of Tahoma. Tahoe City is positioned where the north and west shores meet and the Truckee River begins its journey to Reno by flowing under Fanny Bridge. It is a bustling little community with concerts on the beach in the summer, lots of excellent restaurants, and a few of my favorite cross-country ski equipment shops. Kings Beach sits on the north end of the lake at the intersection of CA 267 and CA 28, an area that gets much less snow than the west shore. It is best known for its long, sandy beach. Incline Village is just over the border in Nevada. With no state income tax, Incline Village is a popular retirement locale for the well-heeled. Tahoe Cross-Country Ski Area is just outside of Tahoe City. Spooner Lake Cross-Country is 13 miles from Incline Village. Northstar is 10 miles from Kings Beach. Squaw Valley and the nordic resort at the Resort at Squaw Creek are 5 miles north of Tahoe City.

Carson City The desert capital of Nevada is a smaller city than Reno, but still big enough to have everything you will need. It is located at the junction of US 50 and US 395, just 10 miles east of Spooner Lake Cross-Country.

South Lake Tahoe Situated right on the California–Nevada border, South Lake Tahoe is the lakeshore's largest community. It is the hub of the Lake Tahoe basin casino action and a place with a very active nightlife. South shore is also close to Emerald Bay and Desolation Wilderness, which offer spectacular summertime hiking possibilities. Spooner Lake Cross-Country is 12 miles away via US 50. Kirkwood Cross-Country is 33 miles to the south.

Mammoth Home of California's largest ski resort and the only major Sierra town between Lake Tahoe and Bishop, Mammoth is a bustling place, loaded with people from the Los Angeles area looking for a winter fix. They can find it at Tamarack Lodge Cross-Country Ski Center, which is just 3 miles from downtown. In the summertime, Mammoth is a hub for outdoor adventures, with several major wilderness areas just a stone's throw away.

Other nearby cities are Bishop, California, about an hour from Mammoth Lakes, and Fresno, California, 65 winding miles west of the Montecito—Sequoia Ski Resort.

How to Enjoy Skiing More

Take a Lesson

Whether you are a first timer or experienced skier, a lesson can really enhance your experience by making skiing easier and more fun. After teaching skate skiing for years, I can tell you that a lot of people make tremendous progress with just one lesson. A few tips, or just the elimination of a bad habit can make a huge difference. Most nordic centers offer daily lessons in both striding and skating and often have clinics to work on specific techniques. Do yourself a favor and take a lesson, and then repeat it once a year to make sure you haven't strayed from the path of good skiing. Even if you are a strong skier, it is a good idea to keep your eyes open for clinics and lessons that can help improve your technique. Learning something new can keep you excited about the sport.

What You Will Learn at Your Lesson

First decide whether to take a striding or skating lesson. If you have never been on skis before and are not sure how comfortable you will be, start out striding. If you have been a downhill skier and have been diagonal

striding at least a few times, perhaps skate skiing is worth a try.

Striding Lesson

You will be taught that classic skiing, also known as diagonal striding, is similar to walking (with really big feet on a slippery surface). Basically, it involves moving your weight from ski to ski while swinging your arms. In a beginning striding class you will probably start with the principles of kick and glide. The kick is when you put your foot down on the snow and then push forward (or kick back). Once you have pushed forward, now you are gliding on the opposite ski. As you get more comfortable on your skis your rhythm will improve and your kick will have more force, helping you glide a longer distance down the tracks. While your legs are kicking and gliding, your arms are swinging back and forth, making plants in the snow with your poles. When you plant your right pole, you should be gliding forward on your left ski. Just remember that your poling and gliding should be opposite. Again, as a beginner it might sound complicated, but once you start doing it you will realize it is quite simple.

Vikings racing in The Great Ski Race

Once you have mastered the basics of walking and poling on skis, your instructor will work on fine tuning your technique. A few things you should keep in mind: Keep your body position slightly forward. Focus on your balance so the weight of your foot is right over your ski (work on those balancing postures in your yoga class). Bend your knees slightly. Keep your eyes forward toward where you are skiing, not looking down at your skis. While on the flats and downhills, keep your skis in the tracks, but to go up steeper hills you may want to come out of the tracks and herringbone. *Herringboning* means that each ski is at a 45-degree angle to vertical; your skis make a V, with the open part of the V toward the front. If you then dig in your inside edges each time you glide, it is easy to stride your way up the hill. For steeper downhills, beginning striders can use a snow-plow technique. The skis are in a V shape, but now the V is open toward you, and when you dig your inside edges into the snow, they will slow you down and eventually stop. Finally, while striding is for the most part a walking motion with arms swinging back and forth, on the flats you can also ski using a technique known as *double poling*. Double poling, as you might guess, means that you plant both poles at the same time and push back. When double poling, keep your skis together and use the poles as the kick.

Many students are comfortable striding after just one lesson, but everyone learns at a different rate. Don't be hard on yourself if you don't pick it up right away. Relax and work on the rhythm of your skiing, and eventually you will have a seamless kick and glide.

Skating Lesson

When skate skiing, instead of striding straight ahead in the tracks, you ski in a wide, flat skating lane with your skis at an angle—similar to the motion your legs make when ice skating or inline skating.

Your skating lesson may begin before you put your skis on. The first step is to get into an athletic stance. Knees are bent and your body position is fairly low, but instead of sticking your butt out, flex your ankles. Think of your body as being in a C shape, or as a Cro-Magnon man. Swing your arms around and grunt a few times if that helps. Before putting your skis on, practice moving your feet from the center and out to the side, alternating from foot to foot. You will discover that a key to skating is that when moving you are almost always on one leg. As your balance gets better and you feel comfortable skiing longer on one leg you will ski faster.

Next put your skis on and get ready to go. Start by falling forward onto your ski, so that if the ski weren't there you would fall on your face. Keep your weight over your ski, then as the glide slows down, fall forward onto the other ski. Like striding, it is all about rhythm and balance. If you are having trouble getting a glide, pretend you are throwing a bucket of water over your ski—that motion will give you forward motion and power. In many classes you will practice the glide without poles for a good portion of the time. This enables you to concentrate on your legs and the glide, because initially the poles can be confusing (and act as a crutch). At least that is what the instructors tell the students; they may just want to watch you suffer.

Once you have learned the basics of the skating glide, it is time to learn about the use of poles. Poling is a very important part of skate skiing. It provides much of the power and helps with the rhythm of the technique. Think of how you use your poles as being similar to changing different gears on a bike. But this bike has only four gears:

First Gear—Diagonal V-Skate This is the granny gear, used for getting up steep hills. Similar to striding, with the diagonal V-skate, you use only one pole on one side at a time. The object is to have your right pole and left ski move at approximately the same time, and then your left pole and your right ski. For me, it is helpful to think of pushing back on my right pole while pushing forward onto to my left ski. Once you get the rhythm down it is a great poling technique that will come in handy when the going gets tough.

Second Gear—V1 This is the primary gear. Many skate skiers use this technique all the time. To V1, push back with both poles at the same time as you glide on one ski, then glide on the other ski without polling, then use both poles and one ski again. Another way to remember it is to think of V1 as "Three One," because on one side you use three (two poles and one ski) and on the other side you use only one (one ski). To begin this technique, start on the side that you will be poling and gliding on. I start on my left side, so I pole and glide on the left side simultaneously, then I pick up my left ski and glide on my right ski without poling. Pole-Skate, Skate, Pole-Skate, Skate. Many skiers find themselves preferring one lead side or the other. Try both and see what works best. If you are comfortable leading on both sides, great! You can then alternate back and forth, spreading out the punishment to both sides of your body. V1 is good for uphills, downhills, and the flats (although I will describe other techniques that also work well on the flats). On long uphills, I have found it helpful to alternate between Diagonal V-skate and V1, as the two techniques use slightly different muscles.

Third Gear—V2 Zoom, zoom, zoom. V2 is the racing gear that is best suited for skiing on flats and gentle uphills. For most beginners, it is too difficult to use on the uphills. V2 is similar to V1 in that you use both poles at the same time, but differs in two ways, which is what makes it so fast. First, instead of poling at the same time as you glide, as in V1, you pole, then put your ski down and glide. Second, instead of poling on one side, you pole on both sides. Pole, Skate, Pole, Skate. The tricky part of learning V2 is poling twice as often. For many beginners getting the timing down can be challenging, and often the skis just can't keep up with the poles, or vice-versa. The solution is to *slow down* and talk to yourself. Learn to glide longer on your ski by saying out loud, "Pole . . . Skate . . . Break . . . Pole . . . Skate . . . Break." Instead of poling faster, glide longer so you don't have to pole so fast. Once you get a handle on it,

V2 is very fast on the flats and very fun. While challenging, it is a good technique for beginners, since it forces longer balancing on one leg. Good balance is a real key to success as a skate skier.

Fourth Gear—V2-Alternate This is the overdrive gear. Most people use V2-Alternate poling when they are skiing V2 and they realize they are skiing too fast or using up too much energy. Just skip every other pole, giving your upper body a bit of a break. Pole, Skate, Skate, Pole, Skate, Skate. I do not teach V2-Alternate to beginners, because it can be confused with V1. Master the other poling techniques, then attempt V2-Alternate. The key is to start out with V2 and switch to V2-Alternate; this will make it less likely that you will be skiing a bad V1.

Other Poling Techniques There are two other ways to use your poles while skating, both of which give your legs a bit of a break. On a gentle downhill you can ski in the tracks and double pole with your skis together. Many large races actually require skate skiers to start out by double poling for the first 100 yards. This allows the skiers to spread out before they attempt to skate and tromp over each other's equipment. You can also ski without using your poles. Once your speed is up to the point that you no longer need them, lift your poles up and continue the skating motion. This is a poling, or non-poling, technique that all skiers should use on a regular basis.

Once you learn the repertoire of poling techniques, you can use the right poling style for the terrain and your speed. Most nordic centers have a series of ups, downs, and flats, so you should have plenty of space to practice all your techniques. I figure that I ski 20 percent of the time diagonal v-skating, 60 percent of the time in V1, and 20 percent of the time in V2. Some strong racers never diagonal v-skate and V2 50 percent of the time. It all depends upon your strength, style, terrain, and personal preference.

After teaching skate skiing to hundreds of people, I can say that the majority of beginners have three challenges:

1. Don't lean back too much. Stay in an athletic stance, think forward and low. People with downhill skiing experience tend to lean back. Don't do it; your butt will be back on your skis and your head will be back on the snow.

2. Bring your feet together in between glides. You are not riding an elephant. Bring your feet all the way back to center before each glide. Many people lose their balance and feel they can find it by getting wider. Instead, try to focus on your core, your center. You have more strength and power if you bring your skis into center and then glide out. One drill to help alleviate this problem is to find a straight line in the snow that heads in the direction you are traveling. As you skate, step on that line with each glide. This will help bring your feet together.

3. Start out with a flat ski, then use your inside edge to push off to the other side. Many beginners have trouble gliding and find their skis sliding out from beneath them. Remind yourself that you need to keep your weight right over that ski with each glide then push off to the other side.

The final thing to do to become an expert skate skier is to ski and ski and ski. It is a tough job but someone has to do it.

Get in Shape

It is important to be in good physical condition before embarking on a cross-country skiing program. While skiing itself is perhaps the best exercise there is, it will help you to enjoy the sport if you regularly exercise before starting. If you bike, run, walk, swim, or do some other form of aerobic exercise at least a few times a week you should be ready to ski. Flexibility and strength are also important. I highly recommend yoga or Pilates to keep your body flexible and strong. Cross-country skiing works all parts of the body, but especially your legs, arms, and lungs, even the core muscles. Cross-country skiing is easier on the body than running and downhill skiing, which tend to be hard on the knees, ankles, and back. While the impact is not bone jarring, cross-country skiing is a weight-bearing exercise that will strengthen your bones and help prevent osteoporosis. For more information on how to improve your physical conditioning, see "Ski in a Race," in chapter three.

If you have been sedentary, before embarking on a cross-country ski program you should talk to your doctor. He or she will probably tell you that cross-country skiing is the best thing you could do, but to take it slow and easy. If you are not in good shape, go gently the first few times out and gradually increase the time you spend on skis. Cross-country skiing should do the following:

- strengthen your legs, arms, shoulders, and core
- increase your aerobic capability
- lower bad cholesterol and raise good cholesterol
- help you lose weight
- reduce stress
- make your teeth whiter
- make you more attractive to members of the opposite sex

So get out there and ski.

Know Your Animals and Plants

In winter, most of the plants are buried in the snow, and many of the animals have settled themselves down for a long winter's nap. But there are still plants to see, as well as a few hearty animals and birds that stay active in the winter months.

Animal tracks at Tahoe Cross-Country

Animals

Coyotes are commonly seen in winter, and they are grateful that nordic centers provide firm, packed snow to travel over while they hunt for squirrels and birds. I have often seen them on the trail at a number of different nordic centers. While black bears are supposed to be hibernating, they are occasionally seen on the trails in the early and late winter. This is especially true in areas they have become habituated to humans, and have become accustomed to the more year-round food supply that we offer via our trash cans. The pine marten is another occasional visitor to the cross-country center trails. These small predators, about the size of a small cat with a long tail, dine on squirrels and birds. A rare treat, they are curious and fun to watch. Bobcats are frequently sighted at Tahoe Cross-Country. Light to dark brown, they are about the size of a large cat, with no tail.

Even if you do not see the animals, the winter is a great time to study footprints. There are numerous books on animal tracks, which often show up nicely in the snow. The tracks often encountered in the Sierra are depicted in my book, *The Tahoe Rim Trail* (Wilderness Press, 2001).

Birds

While many birds fly south or to lower elevations for the winter (because they can) some hearty individuals do spend the winter up in the mountains. One interesting bird, more likely heard than seen, is the blue grouse, a grayish-blue, chicken-sized bird. Often you can unknowingly get quite close to a female grouse before she scares the heck out of you by loudly flying away. The male's mating call is a very low bass *brmmmmm, brmmmmm brmmmmm*. One blue grouse is a legend in Tahoe area nordic racing circles. Several years ago during The Great Ski Race, at about 25 kilometers from the start, I looked up to see a grouse on the trail attacking everyone who skied by. He or she was plucking at the poles and trying to bite legs, and did not look too happy to see a thousand skiers sliding past. The grouse was the talk of the après' ski party, where it was determined that he was attacking people in the front, middle, and back of the pack—he or she was going after skiers for at least three hours. Perhaps he was protecting his territory or she was protecting her nest, but either way it was a grouse that made a lasting impression on hundreds of racers.

Another wintertime bird is Clark's nutcracker. Named after the explorer William Clark, this midsized bird is light gray with black wings and prefers high altitudes. When flying overhead, its wings makes a distinctive *flap, flap, flap*. The nutcracker's call is a grating, almost crowlike caw.

The very common, dark blue Steller's jay, best known for stealing food from campers in summer, hangs around in the winter as well. It is comparable in size to the Clark's nutcracker and has a similarly loud and obnoxious call. Steller's jay nests are often situated in the low branches of fir trees, easy pickin's for a marten, coyote, or larger bird; it is quite surprising the jay is one of the most common birds in the Sierra.

Mountain chickadees are a small, light gray bird with black wings and head. It is frequently seen flitting through the trees. Chickadees are famous for having a call that some say sounds like *cheessse burrr-gerrr*.

Trees

Giant granite massifs and crystal blue lakes are what give the Sierra mountains their stunning visual beauty. I have found, however, that it is the majestic trees that warm your heart. Unique and full of life, they are what

Ancient incense cedar at Tahoe Cross-Country

bring a living dimension to the mountains' beauty. Trees are pastoral peacefulness and a smell of life in an otherwise stark landscape. In winter, while most plants and animals lie dormant, the trees stand out in glorious contrast to the all-white world of snow. When out on your ski, take a break and look at the trees around you.

Incense cedar is like an old bearded wizard. Broad and strong with a shaggy red fur coat, they reach to the sky with big arms and soft, light green needles. Sugar pine is the octopus of trees, long graceful arms spreading out in all directions without rhyme or reason. Long, narrow cone bombs sit at the end of the arms ready to drop on unsuspecting squirrels (or people). If you see the quaking aspen you will know that water is nearby, as they grow only near springs or streams. Its green leaves quake in the wind in summer, turn yellow in fall to provide stunning color, and drop off in winter to show off bright white bark.

Western white pines' big limbs reach up and try to touch the tip of the tree. Near the top are clusters of graceful, narrow cones, like a shorter and narrower version of a sugar pine cone. Even the simpler lodgepole pine stands straight and true, proudly showing off its gray flaky bark and tiny cones. The versatile lodgepole can live almost anywhere, from dry slopes to wet meadows, from 6,000 feet elevation to over 9,000 feet. The ubiquitous fir, the dominant tree in much of the forest, has its own beauty, popping out of a snowy field like a Christmas tree. White firs grow below 7,000 feet; the red-barked red fir grows higher up.

Trees, unlike many other life forms, grow more graceful, more beautiful, and stronger with age. It is the grandmother trees that most attract our attention as they stand dramatically over their more simple progeny. Some, like the Jeffrey pine, almost look like a different species when they reach maturity. The full-grown Jeffrey is incredibly large and powerful. Draped in thick red jigsaw-puzzle bark, its enormous limbs and rounded cones show a grand presence at the edge of a sunny field (or a snowy meadow).

As you move up in altitude the forest becomes a less hospitable place, suitable only to those few trees prepared for its ravages. One resident is the mountain hemlock, found on the north side of ridges in deep snow. Thickly shrouded in dark green foliage, its telltale tip droops over like a wizard's hat, adding whimsy to an already magical tree.

Like the incense cedar, the juniper is covered in red flaky bark, but this tree is gnarled and twisted by the winds, hanging on to life in a rocky crag. Just to show its soft side, the juniper has no cones; instead it sprouts little blue berries that smell like gin. Finally, the highest tree of all, usually found at over 10,000 feet, is the white bark pine. Often gnarled and just a few feet high, it clings to its little bit of soil as the winds and storms pound it relentlessly.

While a joy to behold, the Sierra trees are even more beautiful to listen to. As a storm begins you hear the soft rustle of needles, soothing to the mind and spirit. As the storm increases in fury, the music rises to a crescendo, a freight train roaring through the forest. Lie down, close your eyes and listen to the symphony of sound as the winds rise and fall. Listen to the trees breathe.

Bring the Kids

In *Last Child in the Woods*, Richard Louv writes, "Our society is teaching young people to avoid direct experience in nature." American children are spending less time in nature and more time in front of the television and computer screen. Louv's premise is that not only are children missing one of the best parts of childhood—just playing in the woods—but we are creating a nation of obese, stressed kids who lack an understanding of their natural surroundings. One of the best ways to counteract this trend is to take your children out cross-country skiing. Not only is it a great workout for a generation of children that could really use the exercise, but it is a way to see nature at its best, under the beauty of a soft white blanket.

Some children love cross-country skiing from the start. They can't wait to ski and hardly notice whether it is snowing, raining, or clear, they just want to be out there playing in the snow. Other children, after one cold, miserable day, have had enough and don't want to have anything to do with the sport ever again. And then there is the big group in the middle that may have an interest in skiing, but it is not their favorite outdoor activity right off the bat. These are the kids that need to be treated gingerly, so that they learn that skiing is just playing in the snow. These are the kids to keep dry, warm, and happy so they will want to come back for more.

The Kids' Great Ski Race at Tahoe Cross-Country

There are three things to keep in mind when it comes to cross-country skiing with kids.

1. *The bad news:* They might not like taking lessons. They would just rather go ski and play in the snow.
2. *The good news:* Kids learn fast, and they learn primarily by doing. They will watch you, but don't try to talk to them about body position and what to do with their feet. Just ski with them, have fun, and they will soak it up like a sponge.
3. In general, they would rather ski with their friends than you. So get them into a kids' ski program and let them play in the snow with friends or new friends-to-be. Most nordic centers and communities have such programs. In Tahoe City, the Strider Glider kids cross-country after-school program at Tahoe Cross-Country Ski Area is so popular that there is usually a waiting list. The children's ski programs at Tamarack Cross-Country in Mammoth Lakes and at Tahoe Donner Cross Country are also quite popular.

Children's ability to revel in the joy of play is nowhere more evident than when they are skiing with friends. They don't really like sticking to the trail or fol-lowing a schedule; they want to go fast downhill and then go flying into the powder, or climb up on a snow-covered rock and jump down the other side, or chase their friends and try to trip them with a pole. We can learn a lot watching these kids ski: how to have more confidence when skiing; how to enjoy the snow for the big toy that it is; how to find joy in the little things in life; and to have fun skiing, we just have to be kids again.

You can take your child skiing even before they can walk by using a pulk sled, which are becoming more and more popular for parents of young children. The pulk sled is a small sled that the child sits in, with two metal arms and a hip belt that attaches to the skier at his or her waist. As you ski along, the sled slides along behind you. All that extra weight and sled resistance makes for a real workout, but at least both parents can be out there together, or a single parent can go skiing and watch his or her baby at the same time. Meanwhile, the kids are warm and safe and very likely asleep. As every parent knows, you must leave a sleeping baby sleeping, so now is your chance for a real workout—ski until they wake up!

Wax Those Skis

Wax, but don't stress out about waxing. I talk to a lot of cross-country skiers who know that they should wax their skis, but believe it is too difficult and time consuming. Many have attended a waxing clinic and got the bee-jeebies scared out of them. Some knowledgeable waxing technician told them that waxing skis correctly takes hours of hard work. And don't even get me started on the intricacies of waxing waxable striding skis. Well, I am still not so sure about striding skis, but for skating skis, it is not as difficult as it sounds. Unless you are waxing for a big race and think you may have a shot at winning, the process is pretty simple. First, acquire the following:

- A waxing bench or some other contraption that will hold your ski in place while you wax it.
- A waxing iron. These are available at most nordic shops. They provide a more even heat than that old iron with the holes in it that you can't use on clothes anymore. If push comes to shove, regular irons do work, but don't plan on using it on clothes afterward.

- Several different types of wax. More on this later.
- A plastic scraper to remove the excess wax.
- Some white paper designed for wiping off skis.
- A riling tool. Also available at your local nordic retailer.
- A metal waxing brush.

You may spend a few hundred dollars for all this stuff, but except for the wax it will all last for many years.

Wax

Start out with the basics and expand. For glide waxes (for skate skis, and for the tips and tails of striding skis) start out with purple or blue for cold and dry snow, red for medium temperatures, and yellow for warmer temperatures. For newer snow use hydrocarbon wax, for older and dirty snow use fluorocarbon wax (relatively expensive, so save it for when you really need it). Fluorocarbon wax is also good for those warm spring conditions and comes in low, medium, and very high concentrations. The higher the concentration, the more expensive the wax. For most people low fluorocarbon wax will do the trick. If you are participating in a race and money is no object, then you will probably see some improvement by using the more expensive high fluorocarbon wax.

Waxing Skating Skis and Waxless Striding Skis

Now that you have bought your wax and all of the necessary equipment you are ready to go. The process for waxing skating skis and waxless striding skis is the same except just the tips and tails of striding skis are waxed; leave the patterned area in the center alone. If the snow is very warm and sticky it is probably a good idea to rub on a universal wax on the fish scales in the middle of the striding skis.

Put your skis in the waxing bench or clamps. If the bottoms of your skis are dirty or if you haven't waxed your skis in a long time, start by putting a bit of yellow hydrocarbon wax onto the skis. Some people crayon it on: take the wax, put one side on the hot waxing iron, and then rub the warm, slightly melted side of the wax bar all along the ski. It will feel like you are using a piece of crayon to get the wax onto the bottom of the ski.

A pulk sled: Easy on the child, a great workout for the parent.

Others just drip a little wax all along the ski. Crayoning is more time consuming but uses less wax. Next, slowly move the iron back and forth all along the ski (some waxing experts say to only wax in one direction, but I am not sure why). Keep the iron moving so the ski doesn't get too hot, and take four to five slow passes down the length of the ski until a uniform coating of wax has soaked into the ski. This wax coat is called a cleaning wax. As soon as you are finished, put the iron down and scrape off the wax while it is still hot by taking the plastic scraper and scraping down the length of each ski several times. Use a groove scraping tool to get inside the little groove in the center of the skis, and then scrape along the skis' edges. Once you have scraped off most of the wax, take the brush and brush off more wax, and then wipe the little remaining bits with the white paper.

If you have been waxing frequently and your skis are not dirty, you may be able to skip this step and go on to the next step, which is to put on another coat of wax. This coat is the wax of the day, which should be selected to best fit the skiing conditions of the date and time you will be skiing. Apply the wax to one ski and iron to soak in as you did with the cleaning wax, but this time put the ski aside and let it cool. While the one ski is cooling, go through the process of hot waxing the other ski.

If you have time and don't need to do the final scrape right away, it is a good idea let your skis sit in a warm room for several hours. This helps the ski absorb more of the wax into its base. Some skiers and cross-country ski centers now have hot boxes. You put your skis in a large warm box, usually made of wood, where they sit for a number of hours, soaking in the wax.

When it is time to finish the job, scrape, brush, and polish and you are ready to go. Most people need to rewax after two or three skis.

Waxing really is a fairly simple procedure. If you don't need to clean your skis, and don't feel the need to heat your skis at the end, you should be able to wax, scrape, and polish your skis in less than half an hour. One final step for skating skis is to use your rilling tool to put a row of tiny grooves into the ski, which helps transport water off the skis more quickly, which makes the skis go faster (just believe me, it works). The tool fits over the skis, and then you just press down and make a pass all the way down the ski. Rilling is especially important for older, wet, and warm snows. The warmer and wetter it is, the more aggressively you want to rill. With warm snow you may want to make several good passes down the ski. If it is new, dry snow, too much rilling can slow the ski down.

So you want to wax for a race? Those who like to make sure they go as fast as possible can spend a little more money (okay, a lot more money) and more time. Wax manufacturers like Swix send out a waxing recommendation to nordic ski areas several days before a race, as well as posting them on their Web sites. This recommendation can be a little complicated for the average skier, but you can follow the basics and improve your skis. Their are usually two differences between regular waxing and race waxing: First, often a coat of gray molybdenum wax is recommended for the first wax layer. This hard, messy wax repels dirt and helps keep the next layer of wax from wearing off. Scrape off this wax and brush. Second, a coat of high fluorocarbon wax (this is the expensive stuff) is applied on top, scraped, brushed, and rilled if needed. While it is worth a little extra effort to wax well for a race, don't make it a big deal. Then if you don't win the race, you can blame it on your waxing technique, instead of the fact that you were competing against all those Olympic-caliber athletes. By the way, those folks could take a pair of skis that hadn't been waxed in three months and still be on their second beer by the time us normal humans cross the finish line.

Waxing Waxable Striding Skis

How do you wax waxable striding skis? Wax the tips and tails as you would skating skis. Then deal with the middle of the ski, the "kick zone." This is also known as the "grip zone," and should be marked on your ski when you purchase them. The goal of kick wax is to help the ski to get some traction, or grip, in the snow. Kick waxes, like glide waxes, come in a range of densities for a variety of temperatures: Hard waxes for cold (blue and green), soft waxes for warm (yellow). For icy or warm and wet conditions, when nothing else will work, you might have to use the dreaded klister wax, which provides kick when things are slippery.

The first step to waxing waxable skis is to use a plastic scraper to remove old wax. What can't be scraped off can be removed with wax removing solvent and a paper towel. Next, rub on the appropriate kick wax the length of the wax pocket in the middle of the ski. Then smooth the wax with a foam cork until the wax is almost invisible. Do this several times, adding a thin layer. What about klister? It is nasty, sticky stuff, similar to glue. If you have to use it (although this may be a time to consider using waxless skis instead), spread it on the kick zone with a klister spreader, basically a plastic spatula. Do not rub it in. When you have finished skiing, make sure to remove the gooey mess before it melts all over the glide zone of your skis.

Almost every nordic ski area provides a waxing service. Bring your skis in, drop them off, and the next time you are ready to ski they will be waxed and ready to go. If you would like to wax your own skis, but after reading about it are still wondering what to do, ask the waxing technician if you can watch him or her wax a few skis. You'll soon realize that it actually is quite simple. Well, except for klister.

Ski in a Race

Cross-country citizen races attract a wide range of skiers—from those who have only skied a few times to Olympic-caliber racers—and the cool part is, they are skiing in the same race. The winner of The Great Ski

Will she still be smiling at the top of the hill?

Race in Tahoe City finishes the 30-kilometer course in about 1 hour and 10 minutes, while cruisers at the back can take six hours or more. It doesn't matter how long it takes; the fun comes from participating and joining with a group of other skiers who are trying to do their best. Log on to farwestnordic.org to check out the race schedule, and you will see that a race is going on somewhere in California almost every winter weekend. Course length ranges from 5 to 50 km. Many races are freestyle, allowing both skating and striding, but every year there are a number of striding-only races. There is a race for just about every skier. While racing is often not easy, it is almost always entertaining. At many races the fun begins after the race is over: Most have food, drink, and a chance to regale your fellow skiers with your tales of glory and woe. Some even have bands so you can dance away whatever energy is left. The cross-country racing community is a small, very friendly group. It is a good bunch of people to hang out with.

Not sure whether you are ready to race? Consider it a challenge, not a race. If you enjoyed a sanctioned walk, run, or bike ride, you will be comfortable in a cross-country ski race. The goal is not to win, but to participate. For most people the race becomes a ski about five minutes after the starting gun. The real benefit of a ski race is that once that date is written on the calendar, you have a focus and a goal. If after a few races you decide you love it, but would like to finish a little further up in the standings, then it is time to start working on your technique. Almost every cross-country ski center has clinics and training classes to help improve your skiing.

Training for a Race

When planning to race (or ski, for that matter) during the coming winter, the most important thing to do is improve your physical condition. The first step is to check with your doctor to make sure you are capable of a major new physical undertaking. Your doctor may give you guidelines on how you should train; be sure to follow them. The goal in race training is to gradually build up your endurance and strength, so that you are at your peak when the race begins. Ski training can be divided into three categories: endurance, strength and flexibility, and speed. Look at it as developing slow-twitch muscles (endurance), and fast-twitch muscles (speed and strength), while keeping both sets of muscles flexible.

Endurance (slow-twitch muscles) Since most nordic races take the average skier a few hours to complete, endurance is important. One good piece of news for us over-40 types is that endurance builds up over time. If you train and work on building up your endurance year after year you will become a stronger long-distance skier. Many of the best nordic racers in citizen races are between 40 and 60 years old. They may not beat the young whipper-snappers, but some who have been racing for many years break into the top ten. Endurance comes from staying active year-round. In spring, summer, and fall do whatever aerobic activity keeps you fit—road and mountain biking, running, hiking, fast walking, or gym workouts. In-line skating and roller skiing are also excellent choices, as they mimic the skate-skiing motion. Going up steep hills, whether you are riding, running, or hiking, is especially helpful in building endurance. When winter comes, start skiing slowly, both in pace and duration. Build up to longer, faster trips as the season progresses. The key is to ski regularly and often.

Strength (fast-twitch muscles) The counterpoint to endurance training is strength training. To many people this means spending time in the gym lifting weights. If that works for you, great. Check with a personal trainer or gym instructor for the right type of weight training for cross-country skiing. I like to build my strength the same way I build my flexibility, by going to yoga class. Regular yoga practice builds strength in every muscle in your body—including the major muscles of your arms, legs, and shoulders that are used extensively in cross-country skiing. If you think yoga doesn't build strength, a few minutes in the downward-facing dog or plank poses will change your mind. Whichever strength training method you prefer, it is important to have some sort of flexibility or stretching program going on every day. Whether it is a Pilates or aerobics class, or just doing regular stretching exercises, the more you build strength the more important it is to stretch.

Speed (fast-twitch muscles) While your results in a cross-country ski race are mostly determined by your endurance, uphill sprints and quick starts are also important parts of racing (and skiing fun). Speed comes from training in sprints or intervals. For skiers who race occasionally, the most enjoyable way to increase speed is just to ski fast on a regular basis. Take off and ski as fast as you can for one minute, then do it several more times during your ski when the terrain is suitable. In summer, race up that hill at full speed for a minute or two. Sprinting will help your overall racing ability, and it can be a lot of fun as well. If you haven't skied a V2 as fast as you can on a flat, you haven't discovered the true joy of skate skiing.

Once you have the physical training part down, it is time to focus on mental training. Yogi Berra used to say that baseball is "90 percent mental, the other half is physical." Which is pretty close to the truth about ski racing. Sure you need to get yourself in physical shape, but how you do in a race, and equally importantly, how you feel during the race, can be attributed to your mental approach to the event. A competitive spirit and a refusal to give up are positive attributes for winning a race, or at least doing very well. If winning is not the issue for you, however, relaxing, pacing yourself, and smiling once in a while are also goals to strive for. In my own racing experience, I often feel that my results should be better than they are. Perhaps I do not have the killer instinct needed to move up in the ranks. But if I push myself, but also try to pace myself, I am happy with my results. One final word about the mental part: You can be in perfect physical condition and ski racing is still going to hurt. Your body just wants to stop, but it is in pushing yourself beyond what you thought you could do that you make breakthroughs. And it is those breakthroughs that make you feel pretty good about yourself after the race. At least mentally. Physically, you might be ready for a nap.

Tips for Before, During, and After a Race

It's the week before your first ski race. Now what do you do? Assuming your race is on a Sunday, I have developed a hypothetical training schedule.

Tuesday/Wednesday Treat yourself to a nice long, steady ski. Work yourself, but don't be afraid to take some breaks and enjoy the view. Sprint up a few hills; ski fast on the flats.

Thursday Go for a medium-length ski at a steady, not-too-fast pace. Or, if you are tired and have been skiing a lot, take the day off.

Friday Go for a short, leisurely ski. The goal is to take it easy and have some fun, while keeping limber and in shape.

Saturday Take the day off from skiing. Go to a yoga or stretching class to keep limber. If you can, take a nice little walk. The goal is to keep your muscles alive, but not to wear them out. This is the time to check with the ski area that is holding the race for waxing sugges-

Julie Young pulling ahead of Joe Pace in The Great Ski Race

tions, and then wax your skis. Drink lots of fluids and eat a nice healthy dinner, but nothing too spicy if you are nervous or have a sensitive stomach. Put your skis, boots, poles, gloves, racing bib, water bottle, and whatever you might need in your car the night before, so you won't have to think about it on race day, or worse, arrive at the ski area minus a few necessary items. You might find that it is hard to race without skis.

Sunday Get out of bed at least two hours before the race and have a nice breakfast. Eat enough so you won't be hungry, but not so much as to feel too full. Some racers like oatmeal, some like eggs and toast. Whatever works for you. Drink liquids. Stretch. Go to the bathroom. Arrive at the race location well ahead of time so you can find a parking spot and have plenty of time to arrive at the start. It is not fun to be in a porta-potty when the race gun goes off.

Before the gun goes off, take a deep breath, relax, and remind yourself to have fun. Once the race begins, relax. Pace yourself and save some energy for the end. I remember skiing along during one 20-km race and noticing that a friend that usually beats me by a healthy margin was skiing right next to me. We were both surprised to see each other. Unfortunately, this made me think I was having the race of my life. Actually, it meant that I was starting too fast and later, on a long uphill, I paid the price. It is not much fun to be standing on the side of the course huffing and puffing, watching those you have passed passing you.

After the race, change out of your sweaty clothes and into some comfortable sweats, drink lots of fluids, and have something to eat. Laugh, socialize, and enjoy the after-race festivities. Be sure to pat yourself on the back for a job well done. It doesn't matter if you did better last year or if your time did not meet your expectations. It is over now. Have fun and remind yourself that you did something that most people do not even attempt.

Monday Go for another easy ski and begin to get ready for the next race.

If your reaction to reading this plan was, "Hey, some of us work during the week!" no fear; there are plans for the Monday through Friday nine-to-fivers.

Plan A Quit your job and get your priorities straight: go skiing.

Plan B The weekend before the race, go for a nice long ski. If possible, get an early morning or late after-

Far West Nordic Ski Education Association

The Far West Nordic Ski Association is a nonprofit organization dedicated to training children and adults to be better skiers. They provide training opportunities for elementary, middle school, and high school students in the Truckee and North Tahoe area, as well as Senior Division Skiers (20–29 years old) and Masters (over–30). Mark Nadell, the Nordic Administrator for Far West, says that the goal of the ski association is "to get more people into the sport at whatever age. While a lot of energy goes into our Junior program, we also help the Seniors and Masters be the best skiers they can be." The result of all this hard work has been some spectacular results for Sierra nordic racers, with recent victories in the Junior Olympics and other national races. Many Far West graduates are now leading members of college nordic teams throughout the country.

To assist Far West in their efforts, join the organization. Membership has its privileges, including discounts at most local cross-country ski areas, and regular newsletters on local skiing. Members can also participate in the Sierra Ski Chase, a winter-long series of fun races. For more information, visit www.farwestnordic.org or call 530-587-0304.

noon ski in once during the week. If that is not possible, be sure to get some sort of aerobic exercise several times during the week to keep in shape. Go for a leisurely ski on Saturday and kick butt on Sunday. Don't worry, you will probably beat those of us who over-skiied in preparation for the race.

Know Your Snow

There is a great American myth that Eskimos have 22 or 100 or 1,000 words for *snow* (the number depends on who is spreading the myth). Those in the skiing world have come up with a few choice words as well. A number of factors determine what kind of snow you will encounter when you reach the trailhead, including the temperature when the snow came down, how long it has been since it last snowed, and whether the temperature

Devil's Peak at Royal Gorge

rose above freezing during the day. Over time, as snow thaws and refreezes at night, its consistency changes. If this cycle persists for a few days, the snow tends to be frozen and hard in the morning, turning softer as the day progresses. Cold, dry snow has lots of sharp crystals, which make your skis go slower. Wet snow that has frozen is very fast, while wet snow that is melted and soft is slow and sticky. At groomed ski areas, the snow is affected by the grooming that is performed each day. In springtime, grooming machines operate in the evening, which allows the freshly groomed track to set up overnight. This leaves a nice, smooth, firm surface in the morning. During snowstorms, in order to provide groomed trails, the machines have to go out in the morning, and sometimes keep grooming throughout the day. If it is a major snowstorm, the groomers can't keep up with the snow, and you will be skiing in soft powder, which is great for downhillers, okay for striders, but not so good for skaters.

While I am sure there are a number of sophisticated terms scientists would use for all the different types of snow a skier in the Sierra will encounter (and a few words that cannot be repeated in front of children for the snows of the northeastern U.S.), skiers have developed their own names. Here is my list for the different types of snow a skate skier may encounter in the Sierra Nevada:

Boilerplate This is that rock-solid, shiny as a piece of quartz snow. *Snow* might actually be a misnomer, as it is actually close to ice. Boilerplate occurs early in a ski season when there has not been that much snow yet and even the little snow you received was a few weeks ago, and it is cold. This icy snow is hard to edge and requires you ski right on top of your skis. It can be downright dangerous, especially on steep downhill sections. The only way to avoid boilerplate is to ski later in the day when it has had a chance to soften up. Better yet, stay home and pray for snow.

Hardpack One step from boilerplate toward softness is hardpack. While still firm and icy, you can usually get a bit of an edge and are less likely to slide off the trail into a tree. In springtime, hardpack is often called "crusty" or "morning crust." Skiers who like hardpack call it "fast," as in, "Yeah, the conditions were fast this morning." Skiers who don't like hardpack conditions call it boilerplate.

Firm Next in line on the firmness scale is what I call firm. For skate skiers, firm is usually pretty good skiing. It is hard enough to be fast, but not so hard as to be unforgiving.

Soft and Buttery, Silk, Butter, Just Right, Awesome, Corn The better the snow for skiing, the more names it has, and for cross-country skiing, this is as good as it gets. Not too hard, not too soft, but right in the middle. Goldilocks, who obviously was a big cross-country skier, thinks it is Just Right. Often snow will be very firm, then firm, then just perfect as the day progresses. The just right snow can also be known as butter or silk. It is fast but forgiving and will always put a smile on your face. The problem with Just Right is that it doesn't last long. Once the snow becomes flawless, it soon will change to soft and sticky. In the morning you may ski over every type of snow. Hardpack in the shade of the trees, soft and buttery in some sections where the sun just hit, soft and sticky in the areas that have been sunny all morning.

Soft and Sticky Once the sun really hits the snow it can get very sticky. The right wax can help, but it is best to be off the trails before the snow gets too sticky, as skiing it becomes hard work and not much fun. The initial phase of soft and sticky snow is still pretty fast and fun to ski in, but as the hours progress the snow slowly turns into the dreaded . . .

Glob, Mashed Potatoes, Glue This is the snow that really fits its names. Very soft, dirty, sticky, gluey, messy . . . yeck! Best to avoid if possible. This snow is also known as *Sierra cement*. As with boilerplate, it is time to pray for new snow.

So when your prayers are finally answered and a big storm brings in a fresh new load (also known as a major dump), it is time to experience several other types of snow:

Groomed Powder During or right after a big storm the snow is cold and dry—beautiful but slow conditions for a nordic skier. If you ski both downhill and cross-country, this is the day to hit the downhill slopes, giving the snow a few days to set up on the nordic trails. If there has been more than a foot of snow and the trails have been groomed only once or twice, you may "punch through": skating skis don't stay on the top of the snow, but sink in several inches. Slow, slow, slow. It is a great

workout, however, and if the snow is really coming down, it can be spectacularly beautiful. Just don't expect to set any speed records.

Firm Powder A day or two after the powder, when the snow has been groomed at least a few times, you will find firm powder. The downhill resorts call this *packed powder*, and they still call it packed powder three weeks later when it has progressed to boilerplate. While firm powder is not as fast as hardpack, it has sped up a bit and you will no longer punch through. This is a great time to be skiing. Especially if the trees are still laden with snow and the air is crisp and cool.

Other types of snow:

Off-piste, Corn, or Silk Skate skiing is best done on groomed skating lanes at nordic centers, except for a brief period when the off-piste (off-trail) conditions set up perfectly. If it hasn't snowed in a few weeks, and it is freezing at night and above freezing during the day, the flat meadow off-piste areas can firm up to the point where you can ski all over the sunny, flat areas without sinking. Be sure to take full advantage of these blissful conditions. Some great off-piste skate ski areas include Antone Meadows, Spooner Meadows, open areas at Kirkwood, Euer Valley, Devil's Peak area, and Big Meadow at Montecito-Sequoia.

Sun Cups Late in the spring, after lots of warm days and cold nights without any new snowfall, the snow surface starts to look like a giant golf ball. The sunny flats and slopes are covered with little round dimples known as sun cups. They can be anywhere from a few inches deep to a foot or more. Skiing across a meadow full of sun cups is a rough and bouncy affair, sort of like water skiing outside the wake on a really rough day. Since sun cups occur late in the spring when much of the snow has melted, they are nature's way of telling you to tune up your mountain bike.

Frozen Ruts Ruts are a springtime phenomena caused by the failure of the cross-country center to groom the night before. In the spring, skiers make deep tracks in the mashed potatoes during the day, which freeze into ruts overnight. Ruts can also be caused by snowmobilers who ride over nordic trails after the trails have been groomed. Skiers have a few choice words for these guys and a few places they would like to stick their poles. This is perhaps my least favorite snow condition. The ruts catch your skis and are treacherous. Nordic centers have a cure for frozen ruts: they groom the trails at night and then prohibit skiing after the grooming machines have started working in the evening. My advice for morning skiing in the spring is to ski only those trails that were groomed the night before. My plea to afternoon skiers is to please be off the trails before the machines head out for an evening of grooming. My plea to snowmobiliers is to always stay off nordic trails!

Sugar If snow has been groomed many times and the temperatures are still cold you get sugar. It looks and acts like white sugar granules (except it may not improve the taste of your coffee). While skiing downhill or on the flats through sugar is fun, if the sugar is deep and you are going uphill, it can be a struggle.

Now that you are a snow expert, you can plan your day:

Springtime Get out early, but not too early. You want to make sure you enjoy that brief period of butter, but be close to home by the time it turns to glob.

Midwinter After a big storm, you may want to stride the first day, then skate after that. In the middle of the storm, try to time it so that you follow the grooming machine; the time of day is less important.

Early Winter If there has not been much snow yet and the days are cold, watch out for boilerplate. Ski later in the day and hope for a big dump.

The Sierra Nevada Cross-Country Ski Areas

This section describes the cross-country ski areas in the Sierra Nevada range of California and Nevada. With close to 1,000 kilometers of trails and untold numbers of breathtaking views, I highly recommended you ski all the areas this winter. You are in for a heck of a good time, and possibly a life-altering experience.

The events, races, phone numbers, and Web addresses listed tend to change or are eliminated on a regular basis. Trails are added and subtracted as the years go by. In fact, sometimes resorts close and new ones are established; races are no longer held, or skip a year. Before getting into the car to go to a place you've never been, contact the ski area to make sure they are still in business. A good source for the latest information on races and events is www.farwestnordic.org.

Check the weather and snow conditions before you go. Often television stations, which are heavily sponsored by big downhill resorts, have a tendency to be overly optimistic about the amount of snow that exists in the mountains. Sometimes I feel like the downhill resorts must plow the parking lot and then measure from atop the snow berm. Cross-country ski areas are generally located at lower elevations, so when a downhill area may have snow, the nordic centers are still waiting for the big cold storm. Often a cross-country center will be open, but not have enough snow to groom all of its trails.

In the nordic world, all distances are given in kilometers. The good news is that while 30 kilometers sounds like it must be a harder ski than 18 miles, they are the same. Similarly, an intimidating sounding 10-km race is only 6.2 miles. A piece of cake! The individual cross-country ski areas have provided the distances used in this narrative; distances have not been independently measured. Not all the trails may be groomed or open at the time you arrive. Before venturing out, get a map and ask the ski area staff what trails are groomed and open. While you are at it, ask them which trails are currently in the best condition.

Quick picks are brief descriptions of several of the smaller ski areas with limited operations.

The Lake Tahoe Area

In the area between Donner Summit, about 20 miles north of Lake Tahoe, and Kirkwood, about 25 miles south of Lake Tahoe, you will find seven major cross-country ski centers—America's highest concentration of groomed cross-country skiing. With more than 700 kilometers of groomed trails, you will find everything you could possibly want, from wide open meadows to long, steep climbs, from drop-dead spectacular views of frozen lakes and rocky peaks to deep forests of firs and hemlocks. It's all here for the taking.

Auburn Ski Club

Closest Towns Truckee, CA (8 miles); Tahoe City, CA (21 miles)

Directions *From Truckee:* Drive 8 miles west on Interstate 80 to the Castle Peak Exit and drive to the west end of the Boreal Ski Area parking lot. *From the San Francisco Bay Area and Sacramento:* The Castle Peak Exit is just before the eastbound Rest Stop, at the top of Donner Summit.

Elevation 7,200 to 7,500 feet

Kilometers of Trails 14 km

Contact P.O. Box 829, Soda Springs, CA 95728; 530-426-3313; www.Auburnskiclub.org

The Auburn Ski Club is a unique entity that combines both alpine and nordic skiing. They do not sell tickets; instead you join the club to gain access to the facilities. The primary focus of Auburn Ski Club is the training of young skiers, and many school races and events are held there every year. Located at the top of Donner Summit, the area gets copious amounts of snow, and while there are only 14 km of trails, they are beautifully laid out and almost always well groomed. The club also has a full schedule of clinics and training programs for adults and ski instructors. Training is conducted through the Auburn Ski Club Training Center, which works with every level of skier, from beginners to world-class athletes.

The Auburn Ski Club was formed in 1928 by Wendell Robie, who also developed the Tevis Cup horse race, from Squaw Valley to Auburn and the Robie Equestrian Park, which is located along the route of The Great Ski Race, midway between Tahoe City and Truckee. In 2005 Auburn was voted Best Ski Club in the United States by the United States Ski Association. The

The race is on at Auburn Ski Club (Photo courtesy of Mark Nadell)

High Traverse is the main high trail that winds up and down along the ridge. The **Freeway** parallels nearby I-80, is the closest thing Auburn has to a long, flat trail, and will give you a chance to practice your V2.

Events and Races The Auburn Ski Club is a popular location for middle school and high school races. In fact, in 2005 it was the location of the Junior National Championships for the best 14- to 19-year-old skiers in North America. Over 400 racers attended the event. A variety of different races and events occur at Auburn Ski Club throughout the season. Log on to their Web site for more information.

Summer Bonuses In summer, the nordic trails at Auburn Ski Club become part of a loop leading to and from the Hole-in-the-Ground mountain bike trail. A trailhead for the Pacific Crest Trail and the Donner Lake Rim Trail is located about a half mile away.

Lodging and Restaurants The Boreal Ski Resort has food facilities and a small motel. The Sierra Club's rustic Clair Tappaan Lodge is nearby and provides inexpensive lodging and food. Truckee, 8 miles away, has numerous restaurants, shopping, and lodging opportunities.

club is a nonprofit organization run by a board of directors. Membership is open to all, and members receive access to the training center and social activities, newsletters via e-mail, and eligibility to purchase a cross-country ski pass.

Special Features The training center's nordic facility is housed in a beautiful, 6,000-square-foot building with locker rooms, gathering areas, video meeting room, large sun deck, and restrooms. Just in front of the lodge is a nordic ski competition start and finish stadium and timing building. Other features include a biathlon range, ski jumping hill, and waxing room.

Favorite Trails There are only 14 km of trails, so you may ski the entire network several times, especially if every trail has not been groomed. The trails are short loops that always seem to be going up or down, sometimes fairly steeply—it's a good workout. Several trails provide open views of Castle Peak to the northeast. The

---

Five Reasons to Go to Auburn Ski Club

1. Located right at Donner Summit, this area gets more snow than almost anywhere else in the Sierra, which enables the club to open up sooner than most other ski areas in the region.
2. The club's training programs are designed to help improve everyone's skiing, whether you are 14 or 84 years old.
3. The grooming is usually first rate.
4. At the Western Ski Sport Museum (next to the club), you will find Snowshoe Thompson's huge wooden skis and exhibits about many of the people who have been an important part of the Sierra Nevada's skiing history.
5. With a training program geared towards both alpine and nordic skiers (Boreal Ski Resort is next door and shares the parking lot), you can drop off one child to go downhill skiing, another to join in a kid's training program, and then take off by yourself and enjoy a beautiful day of skiing.

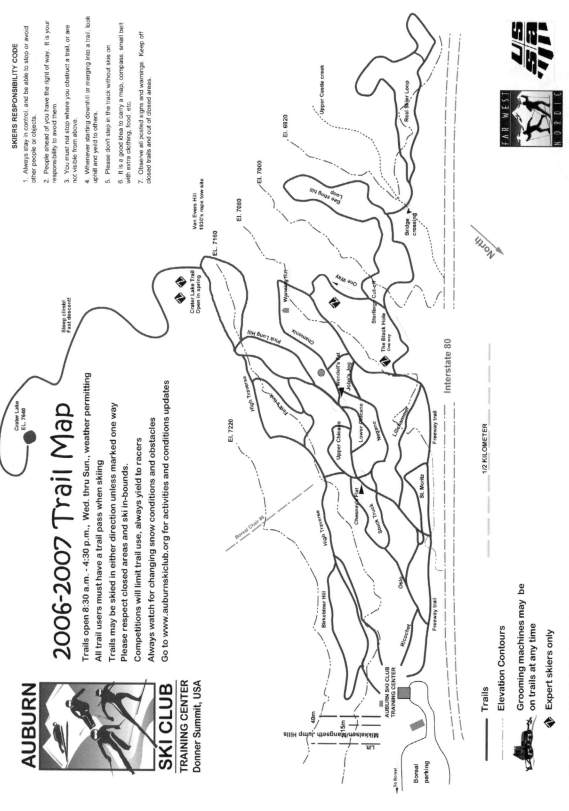

2006-2007 Trail Map

AUBURN SKI CLUB
TRAINING CENTER
Donner Summit, USA

Trails open 8:30 a.m. - 4:30 p.m., Wed. thru Sun., weather permitting

All trail users must have a trail pass when skiing

Trails may be skied in either direction unless marked one way

Please respect closed areas and ski in-bounds.

Competitions will limit trail use, always yield to racers

Always watch for changing snow conditions and obstacles

Go to www.auburnskiclub.org for activities and conditions updates

SKIERS RESPONSIBILITY CODE

1. Always stay in control, and be able to stop or avoid other people or objects.

2. People ahead of you have the right of way. It is your responsibility to avoid them.

3. You must not stop where you obstruct a trail, or are not visible from above.

4. Whenever starting downhill or merging into a trail, look uphill and yield to others.

5. Please don't step in the track without skis on.

6. It is a good idea to carry a map, compass, small belt with extra clothing, food, etc.

7. Observe all posted signs and warnings. Keep off closed trails and out of closed areas.

Trails

Elevation Contours

Grooming machines may be on trails at any time

Expert skiers only

Crater Lake EL. 7640

Van Evers Hill
1930's rope tow site

Crater Lake Trail
Open in spring

Steep climb!
Fast descent!

EL. 7160

EL. 7220

EL. 7080

EL. 7000

El. 6920

Upper Castle creek

Real Skier Loop

Bee Sting Loop

Bridge crossing

Wyoming Run

One Way

Sterling Cut-off

The Black Hole
One way

Chamonix

Pink Lung Hill

High Traverse

Fink's Kink

Wendell's Flat

Jobe's Jog

Upper Chicane

Lower Chicane

Negmo

Lillejammer

Freeway trail

St. Moritz

Stuck Truck

Chesney's Flat

Oslo

High Traverse

Birkebiner Hill

Ricochet

Freeway trail

Interstate 80

North

1/2 KILOMETER

AUBURN SKI CLUB
TRAINING CENTER

Boreal
parking

To Boreal

Lift
Mikkelsen/Mangseth Jump Hills

40m

15m

FAR WEST NORDIC

B. Clark 1-26-07

The Auburn Ski Club Training Center is operated by Auburn Ski Club, Inc.   Nordic programs operated Auburn Ski Club Associates

Map © Auburn Ski Club

Kirkwood Cross-Country Ski Area

Closest Towns Kirkwood Village, CA (1 mile); Meyers, CA (25 miles); South Lake Tahoe, CA (33 miles); Jackson, CA (57 miles); Minden/Gardnerville, NV (35 miles)

Directions *From South Lake Tahoe:* Take CA 89/US 50 south 8 miles to Meyers. Turn left on CA 89 and go south 11 miles to CA 88 in Hope Valley. Turn right and drive west 14 miles to the Kirkwood Cross-Country Ski Area on your right. *From Jackson:* Take CA 88 east 57 miles to Kirkwood Resort on your right, then go an additional several hundred yards to Kirkwood Cross-Country on your left. *From Gardnerville:* From US 395, take NV 756 about 4 miles southwest to CA 88, which you follow west about 30 miles to the Kirkwood Cross-Country Center on your right.

Note Before setting out to Kirkwood be sure and check road conditions. If you are coming from the North Shore of Lake Tahoe, CA 89 at Emerald Bay is frequently closed due to avalanche danger. On CA 88, Carson Pass, which is 5 miles east of Kirkwood and the Carson Spur, which is 2 miles to the west, also frequently close. In my experience these two passes are the most-often closed "year-round" passes in the northern Sierra. The good news is that the reason the passes close is that they get a ton of snow. For road condition information call 800-427-7623.

Elevation 7,800 to 8,600 feet

Kilometers of Trails 80 km

Contact P.O. Box 1, Kirkwood, CA 95646; Cross-Country Center: 209-258-7248, Kirkwood Lodging Services: 1-800-967-7500, Ski Report Hotline: 1-877-Kirkwood; www.kirkwood.com

Located across CA 88 from the Kirkwood downhill resort, Kirkwood Cross-Country has a wide variety of

Beaver Pond Trail at Kirkwood

Giant mountain junipers at Kirkwood

Kirkwood's high-altitude location provides for heavy snow and long seasons. The forest is dominated by lodgepole pine, with red fir, western white pine, hemlock, and aspen also evident. Perhaps the most beautiful trees to be found in the area are the ancient junipers, which are seen throughout the trail system. Many of these gnarled, high-mountain residents sit in rocky outcroppings, looking like huge pieces of slightly browning broccoli. When skiing at Kirkwood you can enjoy a pleasant wilderness feeling with coyotes and Clark nutcrackers often seen on the trails.

Special Features Dogs are allowed on two of the trails. One is a beginner trail that circles the meadow, and the other is the intermediate High Trail, which provides views of the Kirkwood downhill ski area. Signs that provide information about the trees, animals, and the life of Snowshoe Thompson, who regularly skied close to Carson Pass while working for the Pony Express, can be found on several of the trails. There is a lesson area just down from the main lodge and next to it is a short track, known as the Kids Kilometer, with large pictures of animals for children to play around. Kirkwood Cross-Country has three warming huts, one for each trail system. The area has an active snowshoeing program, with full moon treks and the Soup and Shoe program—guides provide hot soup and bread while leading snowshoe trips on the trails.

Favorite Trails The **Dog and Pony** and **Meadow trails** are nearly level trails through the Kirkwood Meadow, a nice warm up for experienced skate skiers or an easy stroll for beginning striders. The views are fabulous and you will feel very confident that you cannot get lost. Since the meadow is surrounded by homes and the expanding downhill ski area, it will certainly not be a wilderness experience, but there is some good skiing to be had.

trails in three separate trail systems. While almost all of the cross-country centers in the Sierra are proud of their beautiful views, it is hard to surpass Kirkwood's vistas of Round Top Mountain, Kirkwood Resort, and the Lava Cliffs. Everywhere you turn the scenery here is truly remarkable and awe inspiring. Just below the rustic day lodge is the main trail system, which includes lots of fun, quick, ups and downs, and of course, great vistas. The Schneider Trailhead, located 2 miles from the main lodge, has a system of trails that lead up, up, and away from the road all the way to Sierra Vista and the Last Roundup Trail. These long steady uphills provide dramatic panoramic views of Round Top Mountain and access to a wonderful secluded bowl above the Last Roundup. Between the Lodge trail system and the Schneider trail system are the connecting one-way trails of Agony and Ecstasy. Try to guess: which ones goes uphill from the lodge? Finally, just across the highway is the Meadow trail system, where 10 km of beginner trails circle the flat meadow adjacent to the downhill resort.

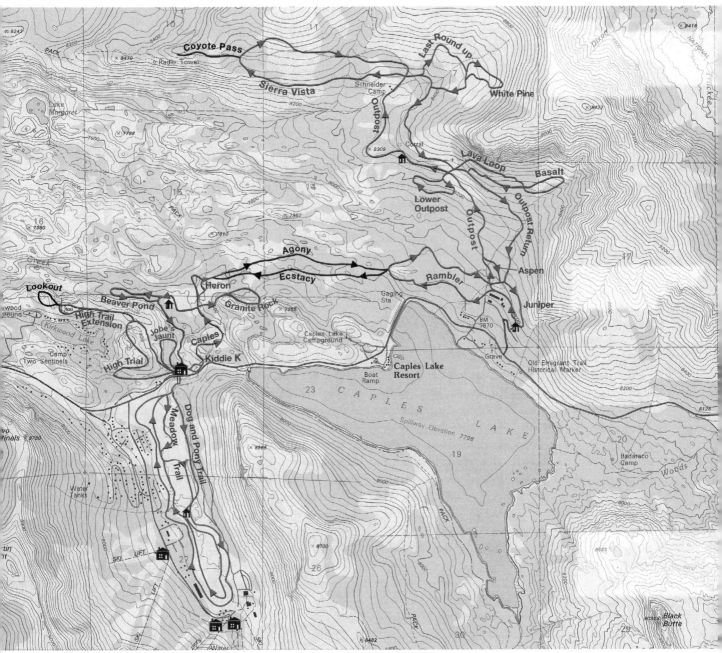

Map © Kirkwood Cross-Country

The trails that head north out of the day lodge on the **Lodge Trail System** tend to be short, with quick turns and short climbs and descents. These trails take you to a variety of terrain and can also provide access to the Schneider Trail System.

The **High Trail** is a wonderful 5-km trail that heads right out from the lodge. Winding up and down through forest and open sections, with great views along the way, it reaches the High Trail Extension, an expert trail that climbs up on a ridge among the juniper trees with 360-degree views. Along this ridge are some short, very steep sections, and then your route returns to the main High Trail. Wind around the ridge, with a few whoop-de-doos and views into the Kirkwood Meadow, to return to the lodge.

Caples to **Granite Rock** and **Beaver Pond** is the primary route down to the main trail system warming hut, switchbacking down a hill with gentle turns to a flat meadow area. From here you can take a quick circle past a big granite rock, named Granite Rock, or head past the warming hut to the beaver pond. The Beaver Pond Trail goes right along the side of a creek. If the creek is running you will get a good idea of the depth of Kirkwood area snows; there is often a ten-foot drop to the water.

Agony and **Ecstasy** are the connecter trails between the Lodge and Schneider trail systems. Each trail is one-way and about 3 km. They wind up (Agony) or down (Ecstasy) a ridgeline above the creek. At the end of Agony you meet Rambler, which connects to the rest of the Schneider trails.

The **Schneider Trail System**, the largest at Kirkwood, has long routes leading steadily uphill with spectacular views of Round Top, Caples Lake, and the volcanic peaks north of the ski area. These trails can be accessed via the Schneider trailhead, 2 miles east of the lodge, or by skiing to the area from the lodge via the Agony Trail, with a return at the end of your day via Ecstasy.

From the Schneider trailhead you can ski on the **Outpost Trail,** a 10-km loop that starts with a moderately steep uphill in the trees, and quickly climbs into an open, south-facing slope with phenomenal views. At the intersection of Outpost and **Lower Outpost** trails is an especially nice viewpoint, with a bench so you can sit and enjoy the sights. The first 100 yards of Lower Outpost is a wide downhill area, designated for downhill practice. Stay on Outpost, and you continue on this open traverse to the Schneider Hut, and then cross over the ridge, ski a few roller-coaster ups and downs in the trees, and reach a large open meadow with the rustically charming Schneider Camp barn. Just a little more climbing past the barn brings you to the 5-km **Sierra Vista Trail.** Here you begin another long, gentle ascent with the views just getting better and better as you climb. At one point you can see from Elephant's Back in the southeast to the Carson Spur in the southwest,

with some of the most beautiful peaks in the Sierra in between. At the end of your westward traverse is **Coyote Pass,** a 4-km out-and-back expert trail. Sierra Vista switches back and heads uphill more steeply east, before a long gentle descent to the **Last Round Up,** 4 km long, my favorite trail at Kirkwood, and one of the prettiest trails you will ever see. It starts with a short uphill and then at a moderate grade circles the side of a huge, open, sparsely treed bowl. It really feels like you are out in the wilderness; I have skied this trail several times and not seen another soul, which enhances that feeling. In springtime this wide bowl makes for some great meadow skating, or telemark skiing. Or just sit down in the snow and revel in the quiet and the beauty. If you still have the energy, before you wind your way back to the Schneider trailhead via **Outpost Return,** try the **White Pine Trail,** a 4-km loop off Last Round Up.

Race The **Echo to Kirkwood Race** is a challenge, with some of the toughest uphills seen in any nordic ski race in the Sierras. It begins at the Echo Summit Sno-Park and roughly follows the route of the Pacific Crest Trail/Tahoe Rim Trail for the first half of the race. This portion of the route is not groomed, just skier packed, and many racers use skins on their skis to get over the difficult climbs. The trail goes by Benwood and Bryan Meadows before crossing over the ridge, and then heads steeply downhill into the Kirkwood Cross-Country Ski Area trails near Schneider Camp. From here the route follows the Outpost, Rambler, Ecstasy, and Caples trails back to a well-deserved finish at the lodge.

Summer Bonuses The Carson Pass–Kirkwood

Five Reasons to Go to Kirkwood

1. The views are spectacular. Even the drive to the trailhead is beautiful. Try the Last Round Up trail or Sierra Vista and you will swear you have died and gone to heaven.
2. It snows a lot at Kirkwood, and it is usually open later in the season than other nordic areas.
3. Kirkwood has a fun trail network with a great variety of trails to match all ability levels.
4. You can ski past a big barn in an old cow camp.
5. When you ski here your downhill skiing friends and family are just a mile away at Kirkwood Resort.

area is loaded with great summer hiking and mountain biking. The Pacific Crest Trail crosses CA 88 at Carson Pass, and then joins the Tahoe Rim Trail just 3 miles north of Carson Pass. Take this trail in late July or August for some of the best wildflower displays in the Tahoe region. The Blue Lakes and Caples Lake are nearby and are well worth a summertime look. A few miles away is Hope Valley, a special place to visit in the fall as it is loaded with aspen trees.

Lodging and Restaurants Kirkwood Resort and village have expanded over the years, and there are a whole host of restaurants and lodging possibilities. South Lake Tahoe is only about 40 minutes away, with restaurant and lodging opportunities too numerous to list. You can even visit a South Lake Tahoe casino and lose some of that money you saved by skipping the downhill resort and going to the nordic center.

Northstar-at-Tahoe™ Resort Cross-Country Ski & Snowshoe Center

Closest Towns Truckee, CA, 5 miles; Kings Beach, CA, 8 miles; Tahoe City, CA, 18 miles. The new Village at Northstar offers shopping and dining close to the trails.

Directions _From Truckee:_ Take CA 267 toward Kings Beach 4 miles to the Northstar entrance on the right. Drive 1 mile on Northstar Drive to the resort. _From Kings Beach:_ Take CA 267 8 miles to the Northstar turnoff on the left, drive 1 mile to the resort.

Elevations 6,800 to 8,000 feet

Kilometers of Trails 40 km

Contact 11025 Pioneer Trail, Suite G100, Truckee, CA 96161; 530-562-2475 or 1-800-Go North; www.northstarattahoe.com

Northstar-at-Tahoe™ Resort Cross-Country Ski & Snowshoe Center is unique among all the nordic centers in this book. While several areas are owned or managed by the same entity that controls a downhill ski area (Kirkwood, Mammoth, and Tahoe Donner) or have trails that are adjacent to or connect to a downhill ski area (Royal Gorge), these cross-country centers are separate entities, operating in their own quiet little world. For better or worse (and it is some of both) Northstar is very much an integral part of the downhill ski area. On the negative side, this means that to ski at the cross-country center you need to park in a large parking lot and take a shuttle or walk a good distance to the Village at Northstar, and then take the Big Springs Express Gondola up to mid-mountain. From here a new lodge is just to your left at the beginning of the cross-country trail network. It could take an additional 30 minutes to get to the skiing than it could at most cross-country centers. So what are the advantages? If several members of the family want to cross-country ski and several others want to downhill, you can all go together and meet for lunch right on the hill. There is a large outdoor deck area to sit and watch the crowds, and a number of restaurant choices (one other negative, those restaurants charge downhill food prices, which are usually quite a bit steeper than nordic area prices). The biggest advantage is that the commute to the trail reduces the number of nordic skiers, so you may have a beautifully groomed trail network practically to yourself. I have waited in line to get on the gondola, skied by the crowds of downhill skiers, and then spent several hours on the freshly groomed skating lanes, seeing only four or five other skiers.

The Sawmill Flat trail system begins just off the gondola at a lodge constructed in 2006. The trails wind through an open forest composed primarily of white

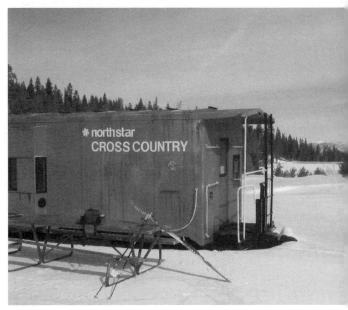

This is one train that is going nowhere, and that is just fine

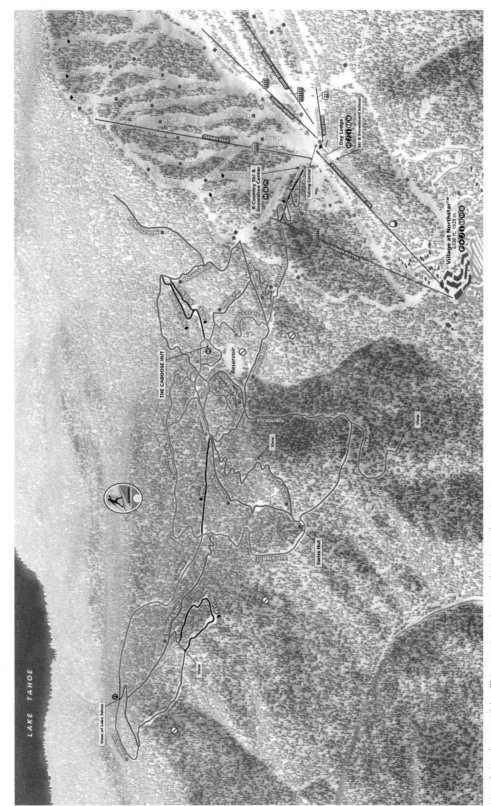

Map © Northstar-at-Tahoe™ Resort Cross-Country Ski & Snowshoe Center

Overlooking Martis Valley from the Swiss Hut at Northstar

and red fir, with an occasional Jeffrey, lodgepole, or western white pine. Views open up on a regular basis of the Northstar downhill trails, Martis Peak and Valley, Donner Summit and Lake Tahoe. Once you have made it to these trails, you are in for a treat.

Special Features Several huts are found at the resort, including a real railroad caboose in an opening next to the Northstar Reservoir. A great place to relax is at the Swiss Hut, a charming wooden hut overlooking Martis Valley. While day ticket prices are high, the season pass rates at Northstar are lower than at most areas. The cross-country center provides light lunches and snacks, rentals, and lessons. The access to the downhill trails make this a great spot to take a telemark lesson, and the area does not disappoint, with a number of telemark clinics held throughout the winter, some geared specifically to women. In midwinter, Northstar also hosts Full Moon Showshoe and Ski Tours. Right at the base of the mountain, the Village at Northstar has grown to include a number of restaurants and most of the amenities you are likely to need. The crown jewel of the resort will be the expansive Ritz-Carlton Hotel, which is scheduled to be completed in 2009, and will be located close to the Big Springs Gondola at mid-mountain.

Favorite Trails Looking for an easy trail out to a relaxing rest stop? Hop on the **Forest Trail,** which switchbacks gently upslope to the **Sawmill Flat Trail,** a wide gentle trail out to the Caboose Hut. From the hut you can take the short **Meadow Trail,** which circles around the meadow and back to the hut. On a sunny day sit at the picnic tables next to the train car and enjoy the view.

The **Lumberjack and Tahoe trails** are longer runs that bring you gently uphill to where a picnic table awaits you. Now you can relax and gaze out at the big blue of Lake Tahoe.

Named after an instructor at Northstar, **Zuniga's Zen** is a really fun 4-km loop with little bit of everything. A moderately steep climb and descent, lots of winding through the trees, and several great viewpoints along the ridgeline at the top of the trail. From the top you can take a quick, actually very quick, black diamond detour onto **Psycho,** which loops back to Zuniga's, or stay on the more moderate Zuniga's Trail back to Lumberjack.

From the Tahoe Trail or Zuniga's Zen take **Castle Peek,** a gentle downhill, to the Swiss Hut, a charming brightly painted wood hut, with views of Martis Valley. The trail then ups and downs its way back to **Woodlands** and finally back to the Caboose Hut.

Events and Races The **Sawmill 15K Race** takes place in late January, and is a highlight of the racing calendar. Once or twice a winter the area between Tahoe Cross-Country, near Tahoe City, and Northstar is groomed to allow skiers to venture from Tahoe City to the Northstar trail network and back. The date varies depending upon weather conditions, but it is always a popular local event. Contact either cross-country center for more information.

Five Reasons to Go to Northstar

1. Beautifully groomed trails that are often lightly used.
2. Wonderful views of Lake Tahoe and Martis Valley.
3. Your downhill skiing friends can meet you for lunch in the middle of the resort.
4. If you are interested in learning how to telemark, Northstar has a program that specifically focuses on teaching that technique.
5. You can spend the night in Northstar and not have to get into your car again until you leave; you will find a variety of activities, lodging, and dining as well as child-care right in the village.

Summer Bonuses Northstar is a summer sports haven with a world-class golf course, downhill and cross-country mountain biking (accessed via two lifts), and hiking on miles of trails. The mountain bike trail network connects to trails that lead to Truckee and the North Shore. The resort also has pools, tennis courts, and other summertime amenities. Lake Tahoe beaches and hiking trails are also close by, and the Tahoe Rim Trail passes within about 5 miles at Brockway Summit.

Lodging and Restaurants If you want restaurants close to your cross-country center this may be the place for you. Just steps away is the Lodge at Big Springs, with a great little take-out place, Chilly Peppers Cantina. There are several other restaurants in the lodge area as well. Back at the village are a number of restaurants, markets, and shops.

Royal Gorge Cross-Country Ski Area

Closest Towns Truckee, CA, 13 miles; Tahoe City, CA, 26 miles; Auburn, CA, 58 miles; Sacramento, CA, 90 miles.

Directions From the intersection of CA 89 and I-80 in Truckee, drive 11 miles west on I-80 to the Soda Springs/Norden exit (about 55 miles east of Auburn on I-80). Drive 1 mile east on Donner Pass Road and turn right at the flashing light (Soda Springs Road). Follow the signs 1 mile and turn right on Pahatsi Road Drive to the end and into the Royal Gorge parking lot.

Elevations 6,700 to 7,480 feet
Kilometers of Trails 30 km

Devil's Peak from Stage Coach Trail at Royal Gorge

The Royal Gorge from Point Mariah at Royal Gorge

Contact P.O. Box 1100, Soda Springs, CA 95728; 530-426-3871; www.royalgorge.com

Here it is, North America's largest cross-country ski resort. When people away from the Sierra Nevada think of cross-country skiing in the Lake Tahoe area, Royal Gorge very well may be what comes to mind. Which makes sense, considering that with 330 km of trails Royal Gorge is at least three times as large as any other nordic ski area in the region. There is a tremendous variety of trails, providing spectacular views, easy meadow skiing, and difficult climbs and descents. You can ski Royal Gorge for four or five days and for the most part ski different trails each day. Situated in an open forest of primarily lodgepole pine, Royal Gorge sits right smack in the middle of one of the heaviest snow areas in North America. This is a full-service resort, which owns the Rainbow Lodge, Ice Lakes Lodge, and the Wilderness Lodge. The Wilderness Lodge burned down in 2004; it will be rebuilt soon after the publication of this book. It

was a large lodge in the center of the trail system that provided package programs including three meals a day, lessons, and an incredibly relaxing experience. In 2005, John Slouber, the original developer of Royal Gorge, sold the resort. The new owners expressed interest in continuing the high standards he set.

As this book was going to press the owners of Royal Gorge introduced plans for a major new development at the area, including a new lodge and about nine hundred housing units in several locations. One of the four "camps" where development will occur will have a new lake and back door access to the nordic trails. Another camp will include three new chairlifts and connect Royal Gorge to nearby Sugar Bowl. The proposal only eliminates a few kilometers of cross-country trails and shuttles between the camps are designed to provide easier access to different sections of the trail network. Perhaps the most intriguing part of the proposal is for The Wilderness Camp. This will include a small num-

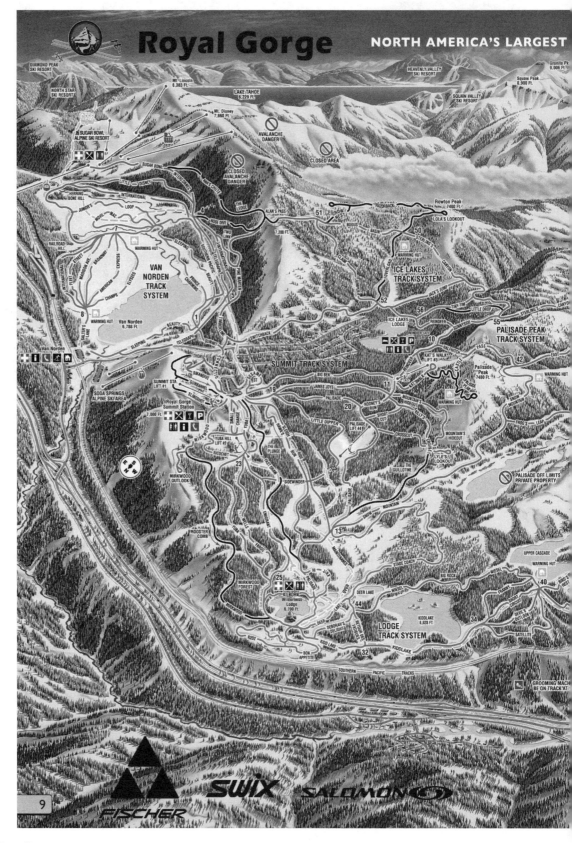

Map © Royal Gorge Cross-Country

Mt. Mildred
8,403 Ft.

Redstar Ridge
6,600 Ft.

Little Bald Mtn.
7,182 Ft.

Maledon Ridge

Snow Mtn.
8,014 Ft.

CLOSED
AVALANCHE
DANGER

The Royal
Gorge
4,417 Ft. Deep

WHITNEY'S
BOWL

POINT MARIAH

BEAR
PASS

WARMING HUT

CLOSED
AVALANCHE
DANGER

Devil's Peak
7,704 Ft.

HORSESHOE

WARMING HUT

THE WALL

KLONDIKE LILT

DEVIL'S PEAK
TRACK SYSTEM

LOOP

TRAIN

WAGON

54

NUMBERS DENOTE TRAIL INTERSECTIONS;
YOU WILL FIND CORRESPONDING NUMBERS ON
TRACK SYSTEM SIGNS FOR ORIENTATION.

GROOMING MACHINES MAY
BE ON TRACK AT ANY TIME

Rainbow Trail open weekends and Holidays only –
dependent upon weather and snow conditions.

RAINBOW INTERCONNECT TRAIL IS
LONGER THAN PORTRAYED IN THIS VIEW.
Distance from Wagon train intersection, #54,
to Rainbow Lodge is 12 km. You may not ski
this trail after 2 PM! One way down to
Rainbow Lodge.

INTERCONNECT

RAINBOW

INTERCONNECT

WARMING HUT

THE WATERFALL

JAMES
NIEHUES

Rainbow Lodge
5,782 Ft.

ber of rustic homes on the far reaches of the trail system, accessible via dirt road in the summer and skis or snowcat in the winter. It may take several years for these plans to become reality. Be sure to check in with Royal Gorge for the latest.

Lodging Rainbow Lodge is located just off I-80, 7 miles west of the main Royal Gorge lodge at Summit Station (take the Rainbow Road exit). Walking into Rainbow is a pleasant trip back in time to a charming 1920s-era lodge, now a rustic bed-and-breakfast, built of wood and rock, with a cozy rock fireplace and excellent dining at the Engadine Café. Packages and discounts are available for those who want to stay at the lodge and ski Royal Gorge. Guests can take the complimentary shuttle to the main trailhead at Summit Station. There is one shuttle in the morning and one back to the lodge in the afternoon. (As this book went to press, the Rainbow Lodge was placed on the market by Royal Gorge. If sold, it will probably still remain a charming bed-and-breakfast close to the trail system.)

Before it burned down, the Wilderness Lodge provided an incredibly relaxing experience. Picture this: You get up in the morning and stretch. Then eat a hearty breakfast, walk 10 feet out the door and ski for a few hours. Come back for a great lunch and then hang out for a bit on a comfy couch in the main lodge. In the afternoon, go for another ski or take a lesson. Come back for a big dinner and then hang out in the hot tub. Repeat this procedure for a few days, no phones or cars or distractions. That was my experience a few years ago, and I am sure that will be the goal for the new lodge once it is rebuilt. Currently there are several cabins that did not burn that are available to rent; one has been converted into an on-trail café.

Just at the edge of Serene Lakes on Donner Summit, Ice Lakes Lodge is a beautiful, bright and sunny mountain lodge. There are 26 lake- and mountain-view rooms, a restaurant and bar, and a guest lounge with floor-to-ceiling fireplace. Purchase tickets at the lodge and walk across the street to the Reindeer Trail to begin a perfect ski day. To get to the Ice Lakes Lodge take Donner Pass Road east from the I-80 exit at Soda Springs to the flashing yellow light and turn right onto Soda Springs Road. Drive 2.5 miles to the Ice Lakes Lodge on your right. This is 1.5 miles past the Pahatsi Road turnoff that takes you to the main Royal Gorge lodge at Summit Station.

Other amenities at Royal Gorge:

- Ten warming huts scattered throughout the trail system.
- Wilderness Lodge Café provides quick refreshment from a log cabin next to the site of the former Wilderness Lodge.
- The Summit Station Café serves lunch fare, such as hamburgers, hot dogs, salads, fruit, ice cream, and drinks in the main lodge.
- The Ice Lakes Lodge Restaurant and Bar is a full-service restaurant, just across the street from the trails.
- Ski over from Summit Station or the Van Norden trailhead on the Sugar Bowl Interconnect trail to join your downhill buddies for lunch at Sugar Bowl Ski Resort. Those who are serious downhill and cross-country skiers can purchase a joint season pass good at both resorts.
- Four surface lifts operate on weekends. These short lifts are located next to wide downhill practice areas, giving you an opportunity to perfect your downhill and telemark skills.
- When the conditions are right (lots of snow and cold temperatures) during a few late-winter weekends the Rainbow Interconnect Trail may be open. If you get the opportunity and are a fairly strong skier, this is a real treat. The trail departs from Wagon Train Trail in the Devil's Peak trail system and goes 12 km on a one-way downhill (mostly) to the Rainbow Lodge. At the lodge, food and a shuttle await you. Summit Station is located at near 7,000 feet; the Rainbow Lodge is at 5,782 feet: this is a significant drop. The low elevation at Rainbow Lodge is also why the trail is only open in a big snow year with lots of cold storms that deposit snow at low elevations. Before starting on the Rainbow Interconnect, ski out to the end of Wagon Train Trail to the Horseshoe Warming Hut. This hut is right at the base of Devil's Peak, and has one of the more inspiring views available at Royal Gorge.

Royal Gorge Trail Systems Royal Gorge is a very big place, with six interconnected trail systems. Many of the longer loops will travel over several of the trail systems, but understanding the basics will help you navigate your way around the area.

The **Van Norden Track System** is located primarily on the meadows surrounding frozen Lake Van Norden. These trails are accessed via the Van Norden trailhead, which is located next to the railroad tracks, about 1 mile before Summit Station. Sometimes the ticket booth is closed, in which case you must purchase tickets at Summit Station. Van Norden trails are a favorite spot for early winter because the trails are located in a low-lying area that tends to stay very cold, and can open with a small amount of snow. Later in the season Van Norden has great beginner and intermediate terrain, and you can ski over to Sugar Bowl via the Sugar Bowl Interconnect Trail. Located in a large open valley, Van Norden can be a very windy place. I believe the fastest I ever skied was skating along on the Van Norden flats with a 30 mph wind at my back.

The **Summit Track System** includes the beginner trails between the Summit Station Main Lodge and the Wilderness Lodge, as well as a few challengers, including the steep Mirkwood Trail. The trails head downhill away from the main lodge for the most part, so be prepared for a climb on the way back. Several trails in this section have lifts available for use on weekends and holidays.

The **Wilderness Lodge Trail System** is located in the vicinity of the Wilderness Lodge and Kidd Lake. These trails make pleasant short loops for those staying at the lodge and are used by other skiers to access the longer routes available at Devil's Peak or Snow Mountain.

The routes at the **Devil's Peak Trail System** take you from the Wilderness Lodge system to the base of Devil's Peak and the Rainbow Interconnect Trail (if open). These longer trails provide spectacular scenery as well as access to the more remote regions of the resort.

Composed of mostly intermediate and advanced routes, **Palisade Peak Trail System** takes you over Palisade Peak and to Point Mariah. From here you will look right into the base of the Royal Gorge, a deep chasm formed by the American River, and be treated to marvelous views of the Sierra Crest.

To the east of Palisade Peak, the north-facing trails of the **Ice Lakes Track System** lead you to Lola's Lookout and the Razorback Trail, which feature awe-inspiring views of Sugar Bowl and the Pacific Crest. Ice Lakes is a great spot for springtime skiing as the cold, north-facing slopes hold the snow longer than other parts of Royal Gorge.

Great Loops The 22-km **Devil's Peak** loop is one of my favorites at Royal Gorge. The views are spectacular, the skiing is challenging (but not too difficult), and you can stop at the Wilderness Lodge Café halfway back to collapse with a Gatorade. The route begins at Summit Station with a fun downhill on the Palisade Trail. Soon you reach the top of the Palisade Lift. Enjoy a little downhill practice on the wide open slope next to the lift and then continue on Palisade to Intersection #13. From here jump on Stage Coach, one of my favorite trails, a beautiful path that winds across an open flat area. In springtime, when you reach the area with views of Devil's Peak, you can take off to the left for some meadow skate skiing before an ascent to a saddle. Then it's a whee of a downhill to Intersection #44. Now it is time to ski through the Boy Scout camp on the Wiesel Trail past Kidd Lake and Big Rock and a last little climb up to the Devil's Peak Warming Hut at Intersection #40. Here the most challenging part of the ski, the Wagon Train Trail, begins. It starts right out with a quick downhill to a low spot, then starts a long, steady uphill to a high point on a knoll just before reaching the Rainbow Interconnect Trail. Past the intersection with the Interconnect you soon reach the junction of Wagon Train and Klondike Lil's. They meet up again in 1 km, so take one trail on the way out and one on the way back. Both routes provide different viewpoints of Devil's Peak, which now soars up right in front of you. At the second intersection of these two trails, head up The Wall on Wagon Train (sounds like a steep hill, but it isn't that bad) to the Horseshoe Warming Hut. Here the views of Devil's Peak are truly sublime. After enjoying the sights you can turn around and retrace your steps, or do the Horseshoe Loop, a very steep expert trail right up to the ridge along Devil's Peak. At the hut, if it is a sunny spring day, there may be more great opportunities for spring skiing on the morning crust. Once you are ready, take Wagon Train back to Intersection #40. From here, take either Short Circuit, Franny, or Satellite down a steep slope to the Kidd Lake Trail, which will take you over the Kidd Lake dam. Next is a small steep uphill that always seems to hurt, because by the time you reach this spot it is late morning or early afternoon, and the snow has softened. The Kidd Lake Trail continues on to the Wilderness Lodge and Café, where food and restrooms are available. One last long, steady, but not too steep uphill awaits you on the Yuba or Wells Fargo trails back to the lodge. Near the top on a weekend you can take the Yuba Hill Lift #2 to ease your way up the last steep section.

The challenging trip to **Point Mariah** takes you to what I believe is the best view at Royal Gorge. Start out at Summit Station and warm up on the almost level Big Ben Trail. Enjoy the flat, as you will be climbing or descending pretty much the rest of the way. At the end of Big Ben, turn onto Reindeer, which you follow through the thick forest above the cabins near Serene Lakes to Half Hitch. Here a short hill leads to the Castle Pass Trail, which you follow to the top of the pass. Congratulations! In just under 4 km you are already at the top of the pass and can begin a steady, sometimes steep, downhill to Intersection #42, where you turn left and take the East Ridge Trail. This downhill can be icy early in the morning. For a more scenic, but quite a bit longer route to the East Ridge Trail, take Palisade to Snow Mountain Trail and ski a long, steady uphill past wonderful views to the Snow Mountain Warming Hut, skiing past the hut to Intersection #42. Start East Ridge with a moderately steep downhill through the trees, then ski out into the open on a flat, before climbing a steady uphill to Intersection #46 and the Bear Pass Trail. Then it's a short, steep climb to a saddle and a short, quick descent to the Mariah Hut and the first of glorious vistas of the Pacific Crest, including Mt. Lincoln (at Sugar Bowl ski area) and Mt. Anderson on the Pacific Crest Trail. After a break at the hut, it is only another kilometer to Point Mariah. The trail goes down and then up steeply before reaching an open flat with views in all directions. To the south and west are Snow Mountain, Devil's Peak, and the Royal Gorge, which drops over 4,400 feet to the American River. To the east is the Sierra Crest encased in deep snow. The Pacific Crest Trail follows the ridgeline between Mt. Lincoln and Tinker's Knob, the little point sticking up to the south of Mt. Anderson. In the springtime the south-facing side of this point holds sun-beaten rocks, perfect for a lunch break or warm place to sit. On your way back, don't be sad, the views are only just beginning. From the Mariah Hut follow Whitney's Bowl as it descends moderately. Catch the lovely panorama to the east of the Sierra Crest. Whitney's Bowl becomes Sterling's Canyon, then continues downhill before a gentle uphill to a junction with the Sunnyside Trail. Sunnyside is the quickest route back to the Summit Station, beginning with a rapid ascent, before heading downhill to Reindeer and Big Ben. For those wanting more, go straight ahead and continue down Sterling's Canyon to a creek crossing, and then begin a very long climb. Just about everyone will be winded after this difficult ascent. When you reach the top, look over Serene Lakes to the west and Castle Peak to the north. From here Sterling's Canyon takes a gentle traverse to the Bogus Basin Hut. Still have lots of energy? Head up to Lola's Lookout, an arduous climb to the ridgetop with tremendous views to the south. Then you can ski Razorback, an expert trail right on the ridgeline, downhill to Crow's Nest and Bogus Basin. If you don't have the energy to take the detour up to Lola's Lookout, continue straight ahead on Bogus Basin, which has a gentle downhill to an intersection with Claim Jumper. From here you can turn right and head to Ana's Chute, one of the steepest downhills at Royal Gorge, providing access to the Van Norden trails. Your route, however, is to turn left on Claim Jumper for a fun, gentle-to-moderate downhill to Intersection #52 and Switchback. Switchback rolls up and down above the Serene Lake's neighborhood to the Summit Connection Trail, which crosses a road, and then ascends steeply back to the lodge. Just before the trail ends at the Summit Station trailhead there is a short downhill past Lift #1.

Events and Races The **California Gold Rush** occurs every year and is one of the state's biggest cross-country ski races. You can race in the 50-km Gold Rush, the 30-km Silver Rush, the 15-km Bronze Rush or the Junior Rush for Kids. The 50-km event attracts top racers from all over the country and is an FIS North America Marathon Cup Race. Between the three races several hundred racers usually participate.

Ski the Huts is a fun event, not a race, but rather a challenge to see how many of the 10 huts within the Royal Gorge trail system you can ski to in a $5^{1/2}$ hour period. At each hut you obtain raffle tickets to be used at the banquet at the end of the event. This is a great way to do a long ski and really learn about the vastness of the Royal Gorge trail system.

Royal Gorge hosts a variety of clinics throughout the ski season, focusing on skating and downhill skills. They also have a very popular clinic for women only,

Ski De Femme. In January the one-day **Introduction to Winter Trails** event allows people to learn about skiing; lessons, rentals, and trail passes are free.

Summer Bonuses In summer, you can stay at the Rainbow Lodge, next to the Yuba River and just a short walk from the trail to the beautiful Loch Leven Lakes. These charming lakes are just a 3-mile hike and by midsummer are great for swimming. The Ice Lakes Lodge sits just above a beach at Serene Lakes and is close to lots of hiking and mountain biking opportunities. Several trailheads for the Pacific Crest Trail (PCT) are located just a few miles away. Hike the PCT 15 miles south from Donner Summit to Squaw Valley for a great ridgeline hike, or head north 7 miles to Paradise Lake, a great backpack or day-hike destination. For mountain biking, try the challenging Hole-in-the-Ground Trail, leaving from the Boreal Ski Area parking lot, or the less difficult Commemorative Emigrant Trail that begins at the Donner Party Picnic Site, 5 miles north of Truckee on CA 89. And if that is not enough, Donner Lake and Lake Tahoe are both just a short drive away.

Lodging and Restaurants Rainbow Lodge's Engadine Café is an excellent choice for breakfast or dinner. Ice Lakes Lodge is another fine-dining alternative for lunch and dinner. There are several restaurants in the Norden and Soda Springs area, including the Summit Restaurant, right at the Soda Springs exit. It sits next door to Sierra Nordic, an excellent cross-country ski shop, so you can eat and get your ski supplies in one easy trip. The bustling community of Truckee is just 20 minutes away.

Spooner Lake Cross-Country

Closest Towns Incline Village, NV, 11 miles; Carson City, NV, 10 miles; South Lake Tahoe, CA, 12 miles

Directions Spooner Lake Cross Country is on NV 28 about 0.5 mile west of the junction of NV 28 and US 50 on Spooner Summit. *From Incline Village:* Drive 11 miles up NV 28 to the Spooner Lake parking lot on your left. *From Carson City:* Take US 50 west 10 miles to the intersection with NV 28. Turn right and drive about a half mile to Spooner Lake on your right.

Elevations 7,000 to 8,500 feet

Kilometers of Trails 80 km

Contact P.O. Box 981, Carson City, NV 89702; 775-749-5349 or 1-888-858-8844; www.spoonerlake .com or www.theflumetrail.com

Looking towards Snow Valley at Spooner Lake

Spooner Lake Cross Country provides access to the heart of Lake Tahoe Nevada State Park. The only nordic ski area along the eastern slope of Lake Tahoe (and the only groomed area in Nevada), it provides easy meadow and lakeshore skiing, as well as some of the longest, most difficult, and incredibly beautiful tours available anywhere. You're going to get a workout, but the skiing is sublime. While the east side of Lake Tahoe tends to get less snow then the west, the folks at Spooner Lake are masters at grooming very little snow. Max Jones and his wife, Patti McMullan, have been running the area for more than 20 years and are both expert skiers who love to put out a top-notch nordic product.

Special Features The Wild Cat and Spooner cabins, which can only be accessed via the nordic trails, are available for rental year-round. Wild Cat is farther from the lodge and has a more private setting. It is small, romantic, and designed for two people (although four can fit "snugly"). The Spooner Cabin is a shorter ski or snowshoe and can accommodate larger groups, up to four adults and two children. Both are charming log cabins in lovely, quiet settings. If you are looking to really get away, one of these cabins just might be the place to do it.

The Spooner Lake Lodge is a charming wood-framed yurt with a woodstove. It has several tables for eating or relaxing, a full rental program, and limited food service. The lodge is a low-key, relaxed place to enjoy your day after skiing. Spooner Lake provides clinics on a regular basis, and gives special discounts on lessons or tickets during the middle of the week.

Favorite Trails Take either **Aspen** or **North Canyon trails** for a long and sometimes steep climb up to a saddle before a fun downhill to **Marlette Lake.** North Canyon steadily winds its way up along a creek; Lower and Upper Aspen Trails journey through groves of aspen trees with views of Snow Valley Peak. Midway through Upper Aspen is the Waterfall, a short, very steep climb. The North Canyon and Upper Aspen trails meet at the bottom of Snow Valley, where the ascent gets steep for the next 1.5 km to the top of the hill, before your descent to Marlette Lake. From the lake you can ski an easy 2.5 km along the shore to the lake's dam, or begin The Big Loop, a grueling 18-km journey past Hobart Reservoir and the infamous Sunflower Hill (more famous in the summer when you are on a bike and you can actually see the mule ears it is named after). This loop is not for the faint of heart or weak of body.

The view from the Marlette Lake Dam on Saint's Rest trail at Spooner Lake

Map © Spooner Lake Cross-Country

Upon your return, skate back up to the top of the hill above Marlette then go back to the lodge via North Canyon or take a ride on Super G.

The difficult **Saints Rest Trail** starts out from the Marlette saddle and winds along the ridgetop with spectacular views of Lake Tahoe before ending up at the Marlette Lake dam. From here follow the Marlette Trail to North Canyon or Super G and back to the lodge. This 22-km loop provides a true wilderness experience and expansive views, similar to what can be seen from the famous Flume Trail mountain biking route in summer. Be prepared for a long and difficult ski with some steep uphills and downhills.

Super G is 2.6 km long and almost all downhill, with wide, sweeping turns, like the downhill race it is named for, that are a real blast. Starting near the summit of the North Canyon Trail, Super G schusses down to the bottom of the Snow Valley meadow, where it rejoins the North Canyon Trail. If you ski up to Marlette Lake, don't miss this trail on the way back. It is always a highlight of my Spooner trips.

The **Lake and Meadow trails,** both close to the lodge, provide gentle beginner skiing, or a chance for a quick, level, warm-up skate. Enjoy the Spooner Lake Trail, which loops all the way around the lake, or ski the mostly level Flying Goose and Spooner Meadow trails.

Lake Tahoe from the Lakeview Trail at Tahoe Cross-Country

In springtime, if the conditions are right, Spooner Meadow can be perfect for meadow skate skiing, and will keep you happily skating back and forth around little melting streambeds. A true pleasure!

Summer Bonuses The Spooner Lake area is a hotbed of summer and fall activity. It is the starting point for the Flume Trail, one of Tahoe's best mountain bike trails, which follows some of the same terrain as the ski trails before traversing along a ridge high above Lake Tahoe. The ski area lodge becomes the home of Flume Trail Mountain Bikes in summer and fall, providing bike rentals, food, and shuttles for riders and hikers. The Tahoe Rim Trail is within a mile of the Spooner Lake parking lot, and can be accessed via a connecter trail around the lake. The TRT heads past Snow Valley Peak and up to Tahoe Meadows on a 23-mile section of trail, or to the south on a 13-mile section to Kingsbury Grade and the Heavenly Valley Ski Area environs. Both sections provide jaw-dropping views of Lake Tahoe. The Spooner Lake area is lush with extensive groves of aspen, making for great fall colors for mountain bikers and hikers. The Wild Cat and Spooner log cabins are available for rent in spring, summer and fall. Finally, a new hiker-only trail parallel to the North Canyon Road Trail was completed in 2006. It wanders through dense groves of aspens and gives the hiker expansive views of Snow Valley Peak.

Lodging and Restaurants Incline Village and Carson City are about 10 miles from the ski area, and both provide a wealth of lodging and eating possibili-ties. Try T's Rotisserie in Incline for great, inexpensive burritos and chicken dishes. South Lake Tahoe is also close, only 12 miles away, where you will find dozens of restaurants that might strike your fancy.

Tahoe Cross-Country Ski Area

Closest Towns Tahoe City, CA, 3 miles; Kings Beach, CA, 7 miles; Truckee, CA, 16 miles

Directions From Tahoe City: Drive 2.5 miles northeast on CA 28 and turn left onto Fabian Way. Turn right onto Village Drive, go to the top of the hill, and veer right. Turn left onto Country Club Drive and Tahoe Cross-Country will be on your left. *From Kings Beach:* Drive west on CA 28. Fabian Way is the first right past the 7-11 on Dollar Hill.

Elevations 6,600 to 7,400 feet

Kilometers of Trails 65 km

Contact P.O. Box 7260, Tahoe City, CA 96145; 530-583-5475; www.tahoexc.org

There has been a cross-country ski area in this location since 1976, when the area began as Tahoe Nordic. In the early 1990s, Tahoe Nordic became Lakeview Cross-Country Ski Area under different management, and then in 1999 the nonprofit Tahoe Cross-Country Ski Education Association took over. Tahoe Cross-Country is truly a community effort, and a community jewel to the people of Tahoe City. For regular skiers it is like the winter post office, a place to meet and greet all of your friends. The down-home atmosphere extends into the lodge, where Kevin and Valli Murnane and their children Lily and Kai run the show.

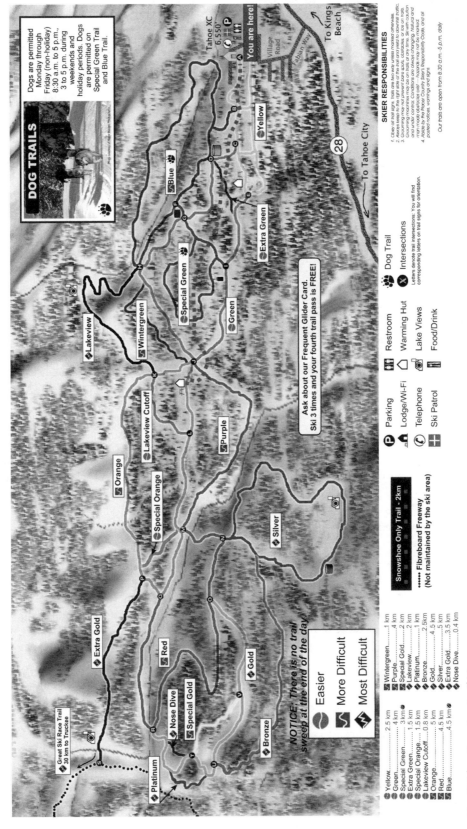

DOG TRAILS

Dogs are permitted Monday through Friday (non-holiday) 8:30 a.m. to 5 p.m. during weekends and holiday periods. Dogs are permitted on Special Green Trail and Blue Trail.

Tahoe XC
6,550

You are here!

Village Road

To Kings Beach

To Tahoe City

28

Blue

Yellow

Extra Green

Special Green

Green

Lakeview

Wintergreen

Lakeview Cutoff

Purple

Orange

Special Orange

Silver

Extra Gold

Red

Nose Dive

Special Gold

Gold

Bronze

Platinum

Great Ski Race Trail
30 km to Truckee

Ask about our Frequent Glider Card. Ski 3 times and your fourth trail pass is FREE!

NOTICE: There is no trail sweep at the end of the day.

Easier

More Difficult

Most Difficult

Yellow	2.5 km
Green	.4 km
Special Green	3 km
Extra Green	1.5 km
Special Orange	1.5 km
Lakeview Cutoff	0.8 km
Orange	.5 km
Red	4.5 km
Blue	4.5 km

Wintergreen	1 km
Purple	.4 km
Special Gold	2 km
Lakeview	2 km
Platinum	1 km
Bronze	2.5km
Gold	4.5 km
Silver	.5 km
Extra Gold	3.5 km
Nose Dive	0.4 km

Snowshoe Only Trail – 2km

•••••• Fibreboard Freeway
(Not maintained by the ski area)

Parking

Lodge/Wi-Fi

Telephone

Ski Patrol

Restroom

Warming Hut

Lake Views

Food/Drink

Dog Trail

Intersections

Letters denote trail intersections. You will find corresponding letters on trail signs for orientation.

SKIER RESPONSIBILITIES

1. Obey all trail signs. Trails are two-way unless marked otherwise.
2. Always keep to the right side of the trail and yield to downhill traffic.
3. Grooming may not prevent bare spots, obstacles, or ice on trails. Grooming machines may be on trails at any time. Ski with caution and under control. Conditions are always changing. Natural and man-made obstacles exist — hazards may not be marked.
4. Abide by the Placer County Skier's Responsibility Code and all posted notices, warnings and signs.

Our trails are open from 8:30 a.m.–5 p.m. daily

Map © Tahoe Cross-Country Ski Area

The Great Ski Race

Tahoe Cross-Country trails run the gamut from beginner to more advanced, with mostly rolling forested terrain. In springtime you can skate out to Antone Meadows, and if the snow has set up just right, skate all around the untracked meadow, often joined by a family of coyotes. Bobcats are also frequently seen, and once early in the ski season, I saw a pair of bears who had not quite got around to hibernating.

Special Features Tahoe Cross-Country has two huts that provide hot chocolate, water, and an escape from storms. Free skate skiing lessons and a variety of different special deals for lessons and rentals are available throughout the week. Season pass holders get "cookie" passes for free cookies and coffee. In addition, Tahoe Cross-Country (often called Tahoe XC) has a very close relationship with its season pass holders. So close, in fact, that they have been known to groom a few trails before and after the ski season, notifying the regulars via e-mail. With some restrictions, dogs are allowed on 8 km of trails. Dog owners are responsible for cleaning up after their dogs and making sure that they are not causing a

nuisance. A separate snowshoe trail winds through the ski area. Four trails provide beautiful views of Lake Tahoe—Silver, Bronze, Extra Gold (The Great Ski Race), and (surprise) Lakeview. A new café was constructed in the lodge in 2006, where you will also find wireless communication (if you must).

Tahoe Cross-Country runs a very active children's skiing program with free skiing for many local schools and nordic racing teams, as well as the Strider/Glider after school program for grades K–5.

Favorite Trails **Silver Trail** is a loop on the outer edge of the trail system, and at the halfway point provides wonderful views of Lake Tahoe. This open and sunny area is a great lunch spot on a warm spring day. The trail follows a gentle downhill of about 2 km to the view and then a variety of ups and downs back to the trailhead. The trail can be skied in either direction, providing a very different ski depending upon which direction you go.

Extra Gold, aka Great Ski Race, follows a portion of The Great Ski Race (the largest nordic race in the western U.S., held every March) route up to the Fiberboard Freeway, a major gravel road through the national forest lands, named after the logging company which once owned much of the land in the area. The trail starts with a steady, 3-km uphill past pleasant tree and mountain views to a lake view at the top, where the trail meets the Fiberboard. From here, the Great Ski Race trail continues, but it is not always groomed for nordic skiing and is heavily used by snowmobilers. Occasionally, with some lucky timing, you will reach the Fiberboard shortly after the nordic center has groomed it. If this is the case, there is a fabulous 5-km climb to the top of Starrett Pass, with an equally fun, long gentle downhill on the way back. Even though the Fiberboard may appear perfectly groomed when you arrive, be prepared for snowmobiles along the route. If the road has not been groomed, turn around and enjoy a wonderful downhill. The best time to ski to the top of Starrett Pass is during the two weeks before The Great Ski Race, when it is groomed more regularly.

While **Gold Trail** is the most difficult at Tahoe Cross-Country, it is only moderately difficult. It involves a long steady uphill, followed by a downhill that is usually a delight. At the top is the open and usually sunny Stump Meadow, a pleasant spot for a well-earned respite. The trail journeys through a beautiful forest of Jeffrey pine, western white pine, and red fir. During periods of low snow, the Gold Trail has some of the driest and deepest snow at the nordic center. Keep your eye open for a pine marten or coyote.

The **Bronze Trail** connects the Silver Trail with the top of the Gold. Whether you are going up or down, it is a fun and challenging route. The downhill includes a series of turns followed by a long, gentle, straight section that is the perfect opportunity to tuck. Be sure and add this trail to your must-ski list.

The backbone of the trail system, the **Red Trail** rolls through forest and along the edge of Antone Meadows. While other trails are feeling the melting effects of spring, the north-facing section of this trail keeps the snow nice and cold. On an early morning in spring, this trail provides access to the freedom of a skate through untracked Antone Meadows. The snow melts and freezes night after night, leaving a nice soft crust, or corn, allowing for skating throughout this large and beautiful meadow.

On that perfect sunny day, just after a fresh snow, take the 25-km **Three Lake View Tour** for the three best lake views at Tahoe Cross-Country. Start by heading out the Yellow and Green trails to the Lakeview Trail. You first meet it at the second intersection of Green and Blue. This Lakeview section is open only in midwinter, when there is plenty of snow. It is the steepest section of trail at Tahoe XC, but fairly short as it winds its way up to the viewpoint. From here the views of Lake Tahoe are panoramic, with most of the lake set out before you to the south. You are also gazing into the heart of Desolation Wilderness and can see Twin Peaks to the west. The trail then has a moderately steep downhill to an intersection with the Orange Trail. If the entire Lakeview Trail is not open, or if the other side sounds a little steep, do an out-and-back from this intersection. If you are

continuing, turn right and follow Orange for several kilometers of rolling up and down (mostly up) to the Great Ski Race/Extra Gold Trail. Now you have a steady, 3-km climb to a lake view, with lovely scenery along the way. If conditions are right, it is a great downhill. Once back on Orange Trail, turn right and follow it downhill to Red. Turn right on Red and ski around serene Antone Meadows, past the Gold Trail and over to Silver (you can add to your workout by taking the Gold Trail up to Bronze, then a fun downhill on Bronze to Silver). Go either left or right on Silver and in a few kilometers you are at another awesome viewpoint, second only to Lakeview as the best at Tahoe XC. Once you have looped around Silver and returned to Red, continue on to its intersection with Orange and Purple. Take your pick (Purple is harder); both lead back to the Green trail and then in a short distance, to the lodge.

Events and Races The **Great Ski Race**, the largest cross-country ski race in the western U.S., often attracts more than 1,000 people. It's a great community event that is the main fundraiser for the Tahoe Nordic Search and Rescue Team. The 30-km freestyle race begins at Tahoe Cross-Country, and after traveling about 8 km there, hits the Fiberboard Freeway and the long, steady uphill to Starrett Pass. From the pass the route is mostly downhill to Truckee, with an especially precipitous drop just before the finish line. When you have finished the race, it is time to start partying with food, drink, and hundreds of skiers regaling you with tall tales of their race adventures. The Great Ski Race is usually held around the first Sunday in March. Visit www.the greatskirace.com for more information.

The Gourmet Ski Tour is a truly decadent combination of skiing and food, featuring gourmet food stations set up along the Yellow Trail; you ski or snowshoe your way from station to station. I believe the little bit of skiing or snowshoeing involved is just so participants do not feel quite so guilty about stuffing themselves with all that luscious food. The event occurs on a weekend in mid-March.

Two other races are held each year. The **Alpenglow 20K** is a fun circuit of the best of the trail system, and the **15K Tahoe City Classic** is just for striders. Check the Tahoe Cross-Country Web site for updates. As the home ski area for North Tahoe Middle and High Schools (which back up to the ski area) the resort often hosts school races as well.

Summer Bonuses During the summer months the area around Tahoe Cross-Country is a mecca for mountain bikers and hikers. A complicated network of trails reaches out from the nordic center, providing miles and miles of some of the best mountain biking in the Tahoe area. While the nordic center is a popular starting point, the trail network can also be accessed from Tahoe City, Brockway Summit, or from the bridge between Alpine Meadows and Squaw Valley on the Truckee River. Most of the trails are suitable for beginners, but there is plenty of more advanced terrain for those seeking a challenge. The Tahoe Rim Trail has trailheads in Tahoe City and on Brockway Summit, and can also be accessed via the nordic center trails. Contact a hike or bike shop in Tahoe City for more information.

Quick Manager's Tip Sign up to have your name placed on Tahoe Cross-Country's e-mail list for weekly updates on special classes, grooming, and events.

Lodging and Restaurants Tahoe Cross-Country's café is a good place for a quick lunch. Tahoe City is just 3 miles away and is loaded with lodging and restaurant alternatives. Try Aspen Grove Deli, or Firesign Café on the west shore for breakfast. Rock's Rotisserie at The Cobblestone in Tahoe City serves up excellent, inexpensive lunches and dinners. For a more elaborate feast go to Sunnyside Resort or Christy Hill.

Tahoe Donner Cross-Country

Closest Towns Truckee, CA, 5 miles; Tahoe City, CA, 20 miles; Reno, NV, 35 miles

Directions From I-80 in Truckee take the Donner Pass Rd exit to Northwoods Boulevard. Drive up Northwoods to the stop sign at the Northwoods Clubhouse, keep going straight for several miles to Fjord and then turn right. You will quickly reach a T at Alder Creek Road, turn left. Drive a half mile to Tahoe Donner Cross-Country on your left. The distance from Donner Pass Road to the ski area is approximately 5 miles.

Elevations 6,600 to 7,729 feet
Kilometers of Trails 113 km
Contact 15275 Alder Creek Rd, Truckee, CA 96161; 530-587-9484; www.tdxc.com

Tahoe Donner Cross-Country is Truckee's hometown cross-country ski area and one of the biggest and best nordic centers in America. Tahoe Donner is a large housing development (one of the largest in the country) that runs the nordic center and its sister downhill resort as an amenity of the development. The ski areas are open to the public, but area residents can obtain discounted tickets. The terrain is extremely varied with lots of steep uphills and long steep downhills, as well as miles of rolling, gentle meadow trails. At Tahoe Donner you can climb 2,000 feet from Euer Valley to the top of Hawk's Peak via the very challenging I'm O.K., Euer O.K. Trail, or you can take a gentle slide around Euer Valley and enjoy the views of the spectacular peaks high above. The large main lodge provides excellent food every day, and in the secluded Euer Valley you will find the Cookhouse, which provides refreshments on weekends and holidays and serves as a large, comfortable warming hut during the week. Tahoe Donner is a popular place for Truckee locals, hundreds of whom purchase season passes and spend the winter skiing the trails.

Special Features On a very limited basis Tahoe Donner provides nighttime skiing on a 2.5-km loop near the lodge. There are five warming huts sprinkled throughout the trail system. The Truckee Donner Parks and Recreation Department and Tahoe Donner Cross-Country have joined forces to produce a kid's program that is active throughout the winter. The center is also home base for the Truckee High School nordic team, a perennial powerhouse. The spacious day lodge provides rentals, retail clothing, waxing supplies, and food. Tahoe Donner has two snowshoe-only trails and two diagonal stride-only trails (but check to make sure they are groomed before heading out). The Downhill Interconnect trail connects the nordic center to the Tahoe Donner downhill ski area next door, and you can then

Cross Country Stats

Number of Trails: 49
Kilometers of Trails: 115
Acres of Terrain: 4,800

Trail Rating:
16 beginner, 24 intermediate, 9 advanced,
2 expert, 2 snowshoe only trails and
2 "Wilderness" trails (Diagonal striding only)

Warming Huts: 5
Track Systems: 3

Elevations:
Day Lodge: 6,600 ft
Euer Valley: 6,500 ft
Hawk's Peak: 7,729 ft

Total Vertical Feet: 1,307 ft

Average Annual Snowfall: 360 inches

Daily Hours: 8:30 a.m. – 5 p.m.

Night Skiing: 5 – 7 p.m. Wednesdays only
December 27 – February 28

No Dogs Allowed

Trail List

Home Range
Meadow Loop	0.5 km
Cup of Tea	1.0 km
Piece of Cake	0.5 km
Night Hawk	1.0 km
Silver Streak	0.6 km
Little Dipper	1.4 km
North Fork	1.4 km
Rough Rider	1.4 km
Pony Express	1.0 km
Lions Leap	1.6 km
Sundance	2.6 km
Boothill	2.1 km
Tumbleweed	1.0 km
White Lightning	2.2 km
Rust Never Sleeps	0.9 km
Dogs in Space	1.8 km
Wombat's Ramble	0.2 km
Big Dipper	1.3 km
Glenn's Gallop (Striding Only)	2.0 km
Firewalker	1.5 km

Sunrise Bowl
Crazy Horse	5.3 km
Drifter	6.0 km
Pegasus	2.0 km
Hawk's Peak	0.3 km
Rolling Thunder	0.7 km
The Far Side	3.3 km
Andromeda	2.6 km
Blue Extra	0.8 km
Hasting's Cutoff	1.0 km
There & Back Again	2.6 km
Snowshow (Snowshoe Only)	2.5 km
I'm OK Euer OK	1.0 km
Downhill Interconnect	3.0 km

This trail connects to the Tahoe Donner Downhill Ski Area. Follow the signs, and with your valid trail pass, you will be allowed one ride on the Eagle Rock chair lift. This will take you to "Mile Run," which you follow and return on the interconnect trail. Please be careful when crossing Skislope Way.

Euer Valley
Hideout	1.6 km
Coyote Crossing	2.7 km
Palute	2.4 km
Broken Spoke	2.4 km
Quick Draw	1.8 km
Cowboy Camp	3.3 km
Barkeater (Striding Only)	5.0 km
Last Round Up	4.0 km
Showdown	2.6 km
High Noon	3.9 km
Ambush	.5 km
That Hoyts	.5 km
Solitude (Snowshoe Only)	1.5 km
Download	0.9 km
California	25.0 km

(Uses portions of existing trails on a track systems.)

Crabtree Canyon	6 km

LEGEND
● Easiest Run	•••• Snowshoe Trail	↷ Steep Curve	ℹ Information	▮ Bar
■ More Difficult	00 Intersection	→ One-Way	✚ Ski Patrol	👁 View Point
◆ Most Difficult	🏠 Warming Hut	•• Diagonal Striding	☎ Phone	🚻 Restrooms
◆ Experts Only	⊘ Closed Area	⋯ Prosser Creek	P Parking	🍴 Dining

the skiing is out there...

Map © Tahoe Donner Cross-Country

Gliding across Euer Valley at Tahoe Donner Cross-Country

take the Eagle Rock chairlift at the downhill resort to the top of the hill before skiing back to Tahoe Donner Cross-Country. The center is also home base for the Truckee High School, a perennial powerhouse,and Truckee's Alder Creek Middle School.

Favorite Trails Just a few kilometers away from the day lodge, the **Sundance** trail follows a nearly treeless ridgeline steadily uphill. With great views of Euer Valley, Frog Lake Cliffs, and Castle Peak, it is a glorious ascent on a sunny morning. After you have climbed enough (or perhaps a little more than enough) that you are ready for a breather you reach **Rolling Thunder,** a thrilling series of switchbacks that loops back down to Sundance. From here you can go to Euer Valley via a quick descent on Firewalker or take the more leisurely downhill on the Last Round-up.

If you are looking for a long, long climb with spectacular views, try **Crazy Horse** to **Drifter.** From the intersection of Sundance and Rolling Thunder, start up Crazy Horse and really start to climb in earnest as you gaze down at Euer Valley far below. Near the saddle you reach an intersection with Blue Extra on your left, a short, easy trail filled with vistas, and I'm O.K., Euer O.K., a precipitous downhill trail to Euer Valley, on your right. Continuing on Crazy Horse, cross over the ridge to expansive views of the Tahoe Donner neighborhoods as well as Mt. Rose in the distance. This fun traverse across the ridgeline and around the slope of the mountain leads to Drifter, at the bottom of a bowl. From here you have one more big steep climb up to the top and a warming hut with views of Donner Summit to the south and into Negro Canyon to the south and west. In summer and fall, a short hike from this hut leads to the Donner Lake Rim Trail (a hiking and mountain bike trail), which drops steeply into Negro Canyon on its way to Summit Lake and Donner Summit. When you are ready, turn around from the top of Drifter for a fun, almost all downhill run back to the lodge. Or for even more of a workout head up a little more to Hawk's Peak, where you meet another junction with the I'm O.K., Euer O.K. trail—from here it is a very long and steep downhill all the way to Euer Valley.

Last Round-up is the main trail that circles **Euer Valley** and offers access to that trail network. A long, gentle downhill leads from the lodge to the valley, where you will find magnificent views in every direction. You can stop at the Cookhouse for a rest or a meal on weekends, then enjoy a gentle ski. Euer Valley is a long, narrow valley surrounded by high peaks. You will ski by a few old cabins as well as a hut next to the meandering stream that splits the valley. Several trails head off Last Round-up to complete your Euer Valley experience. Take the easy Paiute or Broken Spoke, or go for the roller-coaster ups and downs of Showdown. Save a little energy, because once you've enjoyed the Euer Valley trails, it's time for a steady climb back out of the valley to the lodge.

Quick Draw, a perfectly named trail located in a draw, has a series of three quick little drops followed by three quick little uphills. It is a blast that will get your blood pumping. Try it is as your last trail in Euer Valley before heading up the hill and home to the lodge.

Close to the lodge are a series of interconnected loop trails—**Rough Rider, Big Dipper, Little Dipper, Silver Streak,** and **Night Hawk**—that allow for a quick warm-up or a few more kilometers at the end of your ski day. Short climbs and brief, fun descents are the order of the day here. Nice, open views are available from the top of Big Dipper and Rough Rider.

Races Tahoe Donner Cross-Country has an active racing schedule that includes: **The President's Cup,** a 15-km freestyle race, usually held in February (this is the biggest race on the Tahoe Donner schedule); **Sierra Skoogsloppet,** a 15-km freestyle race, usually in mid-January; **Night Races** Wednesdays from mid-January through February; the **Sierra Nordic 3 × 5 Relay,** in which each member of a 3-person team skis 5 km (one skier must diagonal stride), usually in February;

Tour de Euer, a late-season, 25-km tour of Euer Valley with food stops along the way, which is basically a good excuse to ski the best of Tahoe Donner, see a lot of friends, and enjoy some excellent refreshments; and the **Downhill Race Series,** a series of downhill races for

The Good Witch is ahead of the Tin Man and the Cowardly Lion in the Wizard of Oz division of The Great Ski Race

advanced skiers (be warned that these downhill races are certainly *not* for the faint of heart and are recommended for expert downhill skiers only).

Summer Bonuses If you are a resident or guest in Tahoe Donner, you have golf, tennis, swimming, horseback riding, mountain biking, walking, and hiking opportunities within the development. Close by, the Commemorative Emigrant Trail, a popular mountain bike route to Stampede Reservoir, can be accessed via Alder Creek Road in Tahoe Donner or 5 miles north of Truckee on CA 89. A trailhead for the Donner Lake Rim Trail is located on Glacier Way in Tahoe Donner. This trail heads through Negro Canyon to Summit Lake and Donner Summit. Donner Summit has great mountain biking and hiking, including the Pacific Crest Trail. About a half hour away is Tahoe City and the north shore of Lake Tahoe, which provide another big helping of recreational opportunities.

Quick tip Truckee and Tahoe Donner are usually quite cold on spring mornings. This allows you time to have that second cup of coffee before hitting the trails secure in the knowledge that the snow should still be nice and firm. On the other hand, once it does warm up, Truckee gets quite warm, so to avoid the slush; don't have a third cup of coffee.

Lodging and Restaurants Truckee is 5 miles away with numerous restaurants, shops, supermarkets, and

---

Five Reasons To Go to Tahoe Donner Cross-Country

1. This is a great place to go for a long uphill ski followed by a long downhill ski.
2. To have a nice healthy lunch after skiing. It actually makes sense to stay here and eat as opposed to driving into town.
3. To skate around Euer Valley, a remarkably beautiful place. Even though it is close to the lodge, you get a quiet wilderness feeling.
4. Tahoe Donner is the closest nordic ski area to the booming town of Truckee, and every year around 700 people purchase season passes. They must be on to something.
5. It is the only cross-country center that is open for night skiing.

---

motels. Tahoe Donner has thousands of homes and condos, many of which are available for short- or long-term rental.

Quick Pick

Squaw Creek Nordic Center, Squaw Valley

Squaw Creek Nordic (400 Squaw Creek Road, P.O. Box 3333, Olympic Valley, CA 96146; 530-583-6300 ext. 5507; www.squawcreek.com) is an amenity of the Resort at Squaw Creek in Squaw Valley. The Resort has 405 rooms, spa and pools, and shopping, as well as a chairlift that connects it to Squaw Valley USA, home of the 1960 Winter Olympics. Some of the resort's rooms are part of the hotel and some are individually owned condominiums. The Squaw Creek Nordic Center has 18 km of trails that wind through the meadow and forest between the Resort at Squaw Creek and Squaw Valley USA. Most of the trails are on the Squaw Creek Golf Course and are fairly level and easy. The views from these trails to the Squaw Valley Ski area and across the pretty meadow to the homes in the trees, are spectacular.

The Nordic Center is situated in a round yurt, just a few feet from the swimming pools and hot tubs. It is hard to think of another nordic center that allows for such luxurious pampering: A little ski first thing in the morning and then some time in the hot tub? How

The Billy Dutton Uphill Race

The Billy Dutton Uphill Race is held at Squaw Valley USA in early April. In only 5 kilometers you follow the Mountain Run from the base of Squaw Valley to the top of the tram at High Camp—2,000 vertical feet of climbing. It's a killer. The race is open to skiers, snowshoers, and runners. The course is so steep that snowshoers have come close to winning it several times. The skiers pull it off, however, because the last half mile is downhill. In a little over an hour most of the racers have huffed and puffed their way to the top, where they are treated to a buffet breakfast, music, a raffle, and astonishing views from High Camp. After the race you could even go for an ice skate or jump in the hot tub, then take the tram back down. The more adventurous ski back down the race route.

Billy Dutton was a North Tahoe local who died of cancer in 1988 at the age of 39. A member of the Tahoe Nordic Search and Rescue Team, he raced in the first twelve Great Ski Races. Some of his friends still ski or snowshoe the grueling race named after him, which is organized and run by his family. For information contact Squaw Valley USA (530-583-6955).

about a massage or a really good meal at one of the five restaurants?

While the area certainly is attractive if you are staying at the resort, the grooming tends to be a little more hit and miss than at most nordic centers. It is also a popular spot for dog sledding, which makes for great pictures but tends to destroy trails for skiing. Also, unless you are taking advantage of valet parking, you may have a good long walk through the resort to get to the trails.

Mushing in the meadow at Squaw Valley

Northern Sierra Nevada

Mt. Shasta Nordic Center

Closest Towns Mt. Shasta City, CA, 13 miles; McCloud, CA, 10 miles

Directions *From Reno:* Take US 395 north to Susanville, then drive 5 miles on CA 36 to CA 44, which you follow north 47 miles to CA 89 at Old Station. Drive north past McCloud on CA 89 to the ski park turnoff at Snowman's Hill Summit. Follow this road 5 miles to the nordic center lodge and parking area on the left. *From Sacramento or the Bay Area:* Take I-5 past Redding to Mt. Shasta City. Then drive east on CA 89 about 8 miles to Snowman's Hill Summit and turn left at the ski park turnoff. Follow this road 5 miles to the nordic center lodge and parking area on the left.

Elevations 5,220 to 5620 feet

Kilometers of Trails 30 km

Contact P.O. Box 765, Mt. Shasta, CA 96067; 530-926-2142; www.mtshastanordic.org

Put on your skis and set out on the well-groomed trails on a sunny day and you will soon have to stop and marvel at the magic peak looming high above you. Mt. Shasta is a magnificent mountain that captures your attention from almost every trail here at Mt. Shasta Nordic. While the views are certainly the most powerful part of your Shasta experience, it is also just a real joy to ski. The area is small and low key, but with a great trail

Majestic Mount Shasta

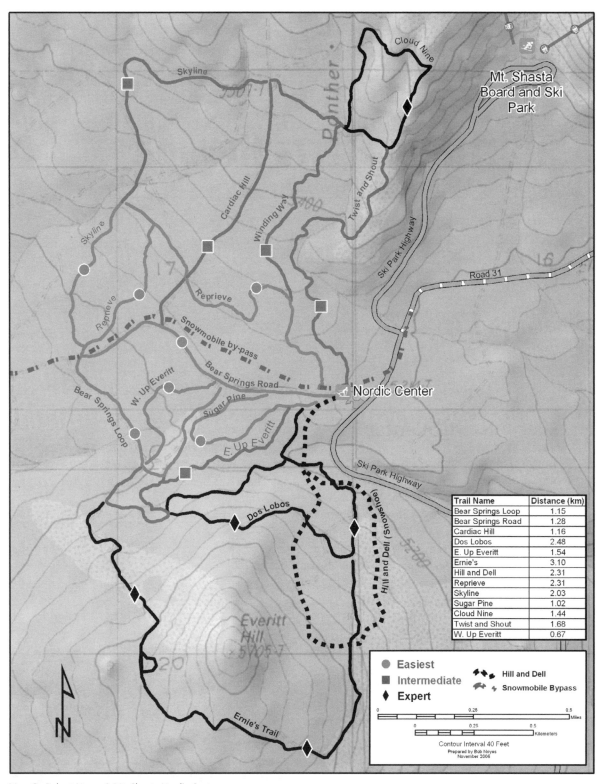

Trail Name	Distance (km)
Bear Springs Loop	1.15
Bear Springs Road	1.28
Cardiac Hill	1.16
Dos Lobos	2.48
E. Up Everitt	1.54
Ernie's	3.10
Hill and Dell	2.31
Reprieve	2.31
Skyline	2.03
Sugar Pine	1.02
Cloud Nine	1.44
Twist and Shout	1.68
W. Up Everitt	0.67

● Easiest   ✦✦ Hill and Dell

■ Intermediate   Snowmobile Bypass

♦ Expert

Contour Interval 40 Feet
Prepared by Bob Noyes
November 2006

Map © Robert Noyes & Mt. Shasta Nordic Center

It's hard not to stop and stare while skiing at Mount Shasta.

network that meets the needs of any skier. Spend three days here and you are bound to have a great time. Operated by the Mt. Shasta Nordic Ski Organization, a non-profit community group, the area is adjacent to the Mt. Shasta Board and Ski Park downhill area, which is a popular destination for Redding and Mt. Shasta area skiers and boarders. While situated at a low altitude for nordic centers in California, it is in the northern end of the state, at the southern end of the Oregon and Washington wet zone. In addition, Mt. Shasta's unique microclimate squeezes lots of cold moisture out of the passing clouds. In many ways, Shasta feels more like Oregon than California.

Special Features Mt. Shasta has wide, well-groomed trails. There is a great teaching area located on a long, nearly level trail right at the trailhead. Picnic tables are situated at a number of sites, providing perfect places to stop and enjoy the view. A snowshoe trail, on which dogs are allowed, wanders through the network of ski trails.

Favorite Trails **Winding Way** leads to **Temple Loop** for a little more climbing before a long, mostly gentle downhill on **Skyline.** This series of trails twist their way uphill to great views of Mt. Shasta and the downhill ski area. Mostly open and out of the trees, on a clear sunny day these trails are a treat.

Ernie's Trail and **Dos Lobos** are highlights of the area. Listed as the most difficult trails, for most they are

There are lots of friendly people at Mt. Shasta

not too challenging. The trails wind and loop through the forest, providing a variety of terrain and views as they traverse around the ridge. Ernie's is not groomed every day; check at the trailhead for current conditions.

The **Bear Springs Loop** and **Sugar Pine Up Everitt** trails loop around close to the lodge. They are easy, short trails with views.

Race The **Ernie Woodfield Memorial XC Tour/ Race** is perhaps the most unusual race you will find on the California cross-country calendar. It is 15 km long, but about half of the course is located off-trail in the backcountry; the other half is on the resort's groomed trails. Many skiers will skate the first groomed section and then switch to striding skis for the balance. Some skiers even set aside a second pair of skate skis for the last groomed section. The winner is a skier who is comfortable skating on groomed trails as well as striding up and down and around backcountry trees. It is a challenging, fun race, with great atmosphere at the finish (and a toast of wine at the beginning). The race is named after Ernie Woodfield, a local character who used to ski here every day in tie-died shirts and other bright clothing. Racers who remember him like to regale other racers with stories of how he frequently rode his bike in the rain, or drove his convertible in the snow (top down, of course). He died doing what he loved best, skiing on the trails, so the folks at Mt. Shasta decided he needed a race to honor him. If you are looking for a different sort of event, with a unique, old-fashioned feel, this is a good excuse to make the drive to Shasta.

Five Reasons to Go to Mt. Shasta Nordic Center

1. Wide, well-groomed trails.
2. Views of Mt. Shasta. It really does take your breath away.
3. Friendly, low-key atmosphere.
4. The opportunity to ski in an area that feels totally different than the other communities and ski areas in California. It is the only place in this book where you will see Douglas fir and knobcone pines along the trail.
5. The charming towns of Mt. Shasta City and McCloud are close by.

Summer Bonuses The Mt. Shasta area is a haven for hiking, mountain biking, mountaineering, and kayaking. Nearby Lake Shasta is the largest body of water in California and is popular with houseboaters, water-skiers, and wakeboarders.

Lodging and Restaurants Mt. Shasta City is just 13 miles away and provides lodging, restaurants, supermarkets, and shopping. It also has some outdoor shops that should be able to take care of any gear needs. McCloud is a smaller community, only 10 miles away, with several restaurants and grocery stores.

Central and Southern Sierra Nevada Region

Bear Valley Cross-Country

Closest Towns Arnold, CA, 26 miles; Angels Camp, CA, 46 miles; Jackson, CA, 73 miles

Directions *From the Bay Area,* take I-580 east to I-205 east to I-5 north to Stockton. From there take CA 4 east 91 miles to Bear Valley. The trip from the Bay Area should take 3 to 4 hours. Once you enter the small village of Bear Valley, the nordic center is the first building on your left, just 50 yards off CA 4. *From Sacramento,* take CA 99 south to Lodi, then CA 12 east 30 miles to CA 49 south. Drive 13 miles on CA 4, and travel 45 miles on 4 to Bear Valley. Depending on traffic it will take you about 2-1/2 to 3 hours to reach Bear Valley.

From Reno and Lake Tahoe, take I-80 or US 50 west to CA 99 south, then to CA 4 east. Or take CA 88 to Jackson, then CA 49 south to CA 4 and head east to Bear Valley. CA 4 between Lake Alpine and Markleeville is closed in the winter (this is east of Bear Valley). While the trip from Lake Tahoe to Bear Valley is a $2^1/2$ hour drive in summer, it will take over 5 hours in winter.

Elevations 7,000 to 7,550 feet

Kilometers of Trails 48 km

Blue Bird Day at Bear Valley

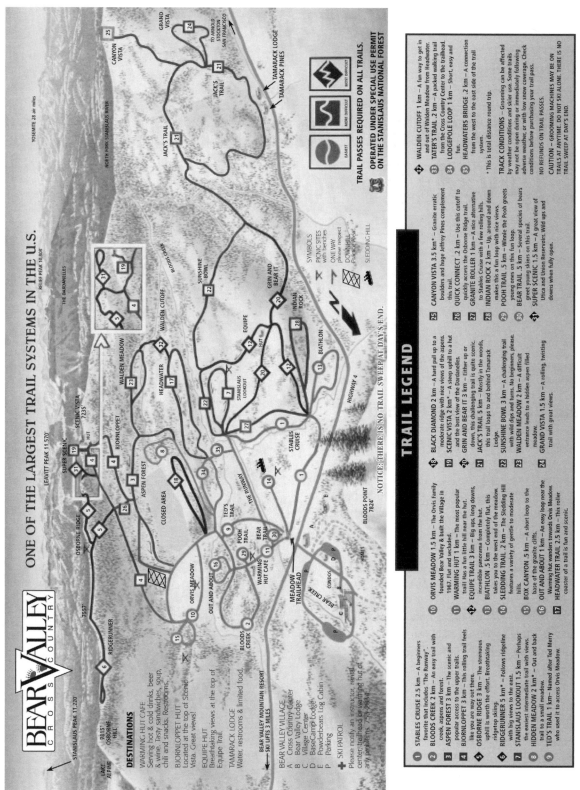

Bear Valley Cross Country

ONE OF THE LARGEST TRAIL SYSTEMS IN THE U.S.

DESTINATIONS

WARMING HUT CAFE – Serving hot & cold drinks, beer & wine. Tasty sandwiches, soup, chili and snacks. Restrooms.

BJORNLOPPET HUT – Located at the top of Scenic Vista. Great views!

EQUIPE HUT – Breathtaking views at the top of Equipe trail.

TAMARACK LODGE – Water, restrooms & limited food.

BEAR VALLEY VILLAGE:
A Cross Country Center
B Bear Valley Lodge
C Village Center
D BaseCamp Lodge
E Powderbears Log Cabin
P Parking
✛ SKI PATROL

Please notify an instructor, rental center, trailhead or warming hut of any problems. 753-2834

TRAIL PASSES REQUIRED ON ALL TRAILS.
OPERATED UNDER SPECIAL USE PERMIT ON THE STANISLAUS NATIONAL FOREST.

NOTICE: THERE IS NO TRAIL SWEEP AT DAY'S END.

SYMBOLS
✕ PICNIC SITES with benches
ONE WAY please respect
DOWNHILL
SLEDDING HILL

TRAIL LEGEND

1 **STABLES CRUISE 2.5 km** – A beginners' favorite that includes "The Runway".

2 **BLOODS CREEK 2 km** – An easy trail with creek, aspens and forest.

3 **ASPEN FOREST 3 km** – The scenic and popular access to the upper trails.

4 **BJORNLOPPET 3 km** – This rolling trail feels like you are way out there.

5 **OSBORNE RIDGE 3 km** – The strenuous uphill is worth the effort. Breathtaking ridgetop skiing.

6 **RIDGERUNNER 5 km*** – Follows ridgeline with big views to the east.

7 **STANISLAUS LOOKOUT 1.5 km** – Perhaps the easiest intermediate trail with views.

8 **HIDDEN MEADOW 2 km*** – Out and back trail to a small meadow.

9 **TED'S TRAIL 1 km** – Named after Ted Merry who used it to access Orvis Meadow.

10 **ORVIS MEADOW 1.5 km** – The Orvis Family founded Bear Valley & built the Village in 1967. Flat and secluded.

11 **WARMING HUT 1 km** – The most popular trail! Has a fun little hill near the hut.

12 **EQUIPE TRAIL 3 km** – Big ups, long downs, incredible panorama from the hut.

13 **BIATHLON .5 km** – Completely flat, this takes you to the west end of the meadow.

14 **SLEDDING TRAIL 2 km** – The Sledding Hill features a variety of gentle to moderate hills.

15 **BOX CANYON .5 km** – A short loop to the base of the granite cliffs.

16 **OUT AND ABOUT 1 km** – An easy loop near the Warming Hut wanders towards Orvis Meadow.

17 **HEADWATER TRAIL 2.5 km** – This roller coaster of a trail is fun and scenic.

18 **BLACK DIAMOND 2 km** – A hard pull up to a moderate ridge with nice views of the aspens.

19 **SCENIC VISTA 2 km*** – A steep uphill to a hut and the best view of the Dardanelles.

20 **GRIN AND BEAR IT 3 km** – Either up or down, this challenging trail is quite scenic.

21 **JACK'S TRAIL 5 km** – Mostly in the woods, this trail loops to and behind Tamarack Lodge.

22 **SUNSHINE BOWL 3 km** – A challenging trail with wild dips and turns. No beginners, please.

23 **WALDEN MEADOW 2 km** – A difficult entrance leads to a hidden aspen filled meadow.

24 **GRAND VISTA 1.5 km** – A rolling, twisting trail with great views.

25 **CANYON VISTA 3.5 km*** – Granite erratic boulders and huge Jeffrey Pines complement this trail.

26 **QUICK CONNECT 2 km** – Use this cutoff to quickly access the Osborne Ridge trail.

27 **GRANITE ROLLER 1 km** – A nice alternative to Stables Cruise with a few rolling hills.

28 **INDIAN ROCK 2 km** – Up, around and down makes this a fun loop with nice views.

29 **POOH TRAIL .5 km** – Winnie the Pooh greets young ones on this fun loop.

30 **BEAR TRAIL .5 km** – Several species of bears greet young skiers on this trail.

SUPER SCENIC 1.5 km – A great view of Utica and Union Reservoirs. Wild ups and downs when fully open.

WALDEN CUTOFF 1 km – A fun way to get in and out of Walden Meadow from Headwater.

33 **TATER'S TRAIL .2 km** – A packed walking trail from the Cross Country Center to the trailhead.

34 **LODGEPOLE LOOP 1 km** – Short, easy and fun.

35 **HEADWATERS BRIDGE .2 km** – A connection from the west to the east side of the trail system.

* This is total distance round trip.

TRACK CONDITIONS – Grooming can be affected by weather conditions and skier use. Some trails may not be open during or immediately following adverse weather, or with low snow coverage. Check conditions before purchasing your trail pass.

NO REFUNDS ON TRAIL PASSES.

CAUTION – GROOMING MACHINES MAY BE ON TRAILS AT ANYTIME. DO NOT SKI ALONE. THERE IS NO TRAIL SWEEP AT DAY'S END.

Map © Bear Valley Cross-Country

Awesome views from Equipe Trail at Bear Valley

Contact Bear Valley Cross-Country and Adventure Company, 1 Bear Valley Rd, P.O. Box 5120, Bear Valley, CA 95223; 209-753-2834; www.bear valleyxc.com

Driving from Lake Tahoe to Bear Valley in winter is a long trip. On the way, I remember thinking, this is a long way to go to ski. After arriving and spending two wonderful midweek days, however, I realized it was worth the drive. This is a very special place with optimum terrain for a cross-country ski center. There are lots of gentle trails winding through aspen meadows, as well as challenging ascents and descents for the more experienced skiers. Everywhere you go you find monumental views. Some trails are sheltered in the trees and excellent for cold and windy days, while others are exposed and perfect for a sunny day in spring. The Bear Valley Cross-Country lodge is located in a large building with gift shop, rental shop, and small food area. It is also the town gas station and is located just a few hundred yards from the charming little village that is Bear Valley. A few shops, a few restaurants, and a few bars make up Bear Valley, and that's enough. It's a bit like going back in time, and on a snowy evening you will feel there is no place else on earth you would rather be.

Special Features Bear Valley has three warming huts, two roomy ones that supply water and views, and a third that includes a café providing grilled burgers, sandwiches, hot and cold drinks, and restrooms. At one end of the trail system is Tamarack Lodge, which in addition to lodging, offers water, restrooms, and limited food. There are picnic tables and benches throughout the trail system, just waiting for you to take a break on a sunny day. For children there are several kid's trails and cutout characters to ski through, as well as a trade-up ski program—buy ski equipment for your children and then trade up to new gear at no additional cost as your children grow. In early winter, a wine tour takes place on the trails; in spring a gourmet tour features food from local restaurants at stations throughout the trail system. Bear Valley has its own groomed sledding hill; you can even rent sleds. A nice touch is the trail map that, in addition to distances, provides a brief description of each trail. The center keeps things interesting with a whole series of winter events, from full moon ski tours to winterfest activities. Be sure to give them a call, or keep tabs on the latest information via their Web site.

Favorite Trails **Sunrise Bowl, Grin and Bear It,** and **Equipe** are three intermediate trails that form a loop, unrolling in a series of ups and downs through a mostly open forest of lodgepole, juniper, and Jeffrey pine. The trails are often sun drenched and you can enjoy the beautiful views. Sunrise Bowl travels down along a creek and then dumps out at the bottom of Grin and Bear It. You will soon discover where it got its name as you struggle back up the hill to an intersection with Equipe Trail.

Ted's Trail, Orvis Meadow, Out and About, and **Blood's Creek** are short loops that revolve around the Warming Hut Café in the meadow area. These easy trails are perfect for beginners, but all skiers will have fun and enjoy the views.

Loop your way through **Aspen Forest, Walden Meadow, Walden Cut-off,** and **Headwater** to find beautiful groves of aspens, entertaining rolling sections, and excellent mountain and meadow views. The Walden Meadow trail is a special treat, with a small loop through gigantic aspens.

Bjornloppet is a long loop trail and the centerpiece of the Bjornloppet Race, held every year. A steep climb is followed by a gentler traverse through the firs and aspens. It is fun, intermediate terrain, and the route provides access to the highest trails in the Bear Valley system.

Scenic Vista, Osborne Ridge, and **Ridgerunner** sit at the top of a ridge and provide panoramic views of the surrounding mountains. Take the short, steep climb on Scenic Vista to the Bjornloppet Hut for expansive views of the Dardanelles. Osborne Ridge starts with a long, steep uphill to Ridgerunner, where you zip along the top of the ridge (imagine that!).

Indian Rock is a short, fun trail with some good climbs, quick descents, and excellent views.

Begin with the gentle meadow glide of **Stables Cruise,** then step it up a bit on **Granite Roller** before hitting the **Runway**. This wide, perfectly straight trail is named correctly not only because it looks like an airport runway, but because it is the location of an airport landing strip in summer months. This is a great spot to try out your V2 technique or take a lesson.

Races The **Bjornloppet** is a 20-km race, and a popular destination on the Sierra cross-country racing circuit for over 30 years. It is usually held in mid-March as part of a full weekend of ski activities. **Tom's Race** is Bear Valley's 10-km striding race, usually held around the first of April.

Summer Bonuses Bear Valley is located at 7,000 feet in the heart of the Sierra, and is a haven for outdoor activity in all seasons. The Pacific Crest Trail crosses

Bear Valley

CA 4 just a few miles to the east. Lakes and streams for kayaking abound in the area and Lake Tahoe and Markleeville are just a short drive away. Bear Valley Cross-Country rents mountain bikes and kayak gear in summer.

Lodging and Restaurants Bear Valley is home to Basecamp, Bear Valley, and Tamarack lodges. The cross-country center has teamed up with the lodge and other area establishments to offer midweek ski and lodging packages. There are several restaurants in Bear Valley. The town of Arnold, which has more extensive restaurant choices, is located 26 miles away.

Tamarack Cross-Country Ski Center at Mammoth Mountain

Closest Towns Mammoth Lakes, CA, 2 miles; June Lake, CA, 17 miles; Bishop, CA, 44 miles

Directions From the Reno area: Drive south on I- 395 about 165 miles to CA 203, the Mammoth Lakes turnoff. *From North Lake Tahoe:* Take CA 28 east to Spooner Summit, then US 50 east to Carson City, and then take I-395 south to Mammoth. *From South Lake Tahoe:* Take Kingsbury Grade to Minden/Gardnerville and then I-395 south.

Five Reasons to Go to Bear Valley Cross-Country

1. Awesome nordic skiing terrain; something for everyone and you will never get bored.
2. The Warming Hut Café. Enjoy a great meal outdoors on the sunny deck, or huddled inside on a snowy day. It's close to the trailhead, but far enough away to feel far away.
3. Bear Valley is a charming village with lots of friendly people, a relaxing place to spend a few days. Park your car and forget about it until it is time to drive home. Stay at the Basecamp for a rustic and inexpensive lodging and dining experience.
4. Bear Valley Mountain Resort is 3 miles away, for those who also want to downhill ski.
5. Dual striding tracks next to the skating lane, for those who like to stride with friends.

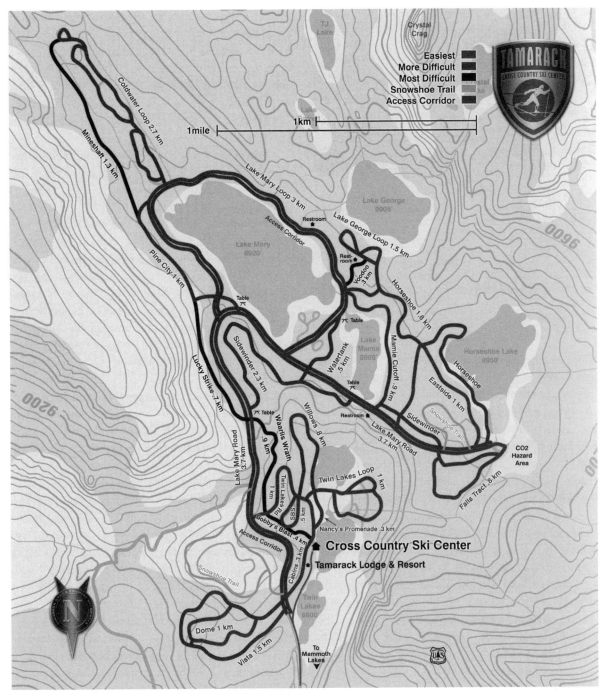

Map © Tamarack Cross-Country Ski Center at Mammoth Mountain

From the Bay Area In winter, most mountain passes near Mammoth are closed. The three routes available to Bay Area drivers are as follows: 1. drive east on CA 88 past Kirkwood and out to Minden, NV, then take I-395 south; 2. drive east on US 50 to South Lake Tahoe, and then just past the casinos at the California–Nevada border take Kingsbury Grade to Minden, NV, and I-395 south; or 3. drive east on I-80 to Truckee, then CA 267 to

Lake Mary at Tamarack Cross Country in Mammoth

Kings Beach. Turn left and take CA/NV 28 east to Spooner Summit, and then left onto US 50 to Carson City. Next head south on I-395 to Mammoth Lakes.

If you have not had the opportunity to drive I-395 you are in for a treat. Whether you catch it from Southern California, or from US 50 or CA 88 in the north, the views of the high peaks of the Sierra are absolutely sublime, especially in the area between Bridgeport and Lone Pine. No matter how many times I see it, I am amazed at how dramatically beautiful it is. But keep one eye on the road, and look for the Mammoth Lakes turnoff. From there, drive through Mammoth Lakes on CA 203. At the second stoplight go straight on to Lake Mary Road and head uphill about 2 miles. Once you go through a tunnel underneath a Mammoth Mountain ski run you are getting close. The road dead-ends at the Tamarack Lodge and Cross-Country Ski Area.

Elevations 8,600 to 9,000 feet

Kilometers of Trails 45 km

Contact P.O. Box 69, Mammoth Lakes, CA 93456; 760-934-2442 or 1-800-Mammoth; www.mammoth mountain.com

Mammoth's cross-country ski area sits in the center of the high peaks of the southern Sierra in an area blessed with copious amounts of snow. The trail system winds through a summertime resort and camping area past several spectacular, usually frozen, lakes known as the Mammoth Lakes Basin. As you slide past Lake Mary, Lake George, and Horseshoe Lake you will be stunned by awesome sights of the Pacific Crest, the John Muir and Ansel Adams wilderness areas towering high above you. Situated next door to the nordic center is the Tamarack Lodge, a rustic inn with rooms and cabins located right on the ski trails.

Special Features You can literally ski right out the door of your cabin at Tamarack Lodge, or enjoy fine dining at the Lakefront Restaurant. Free shuttles travel several times a day from downtown Mammoth Lakes up to the nordic center. The area also provides full-moon snowshoe tours from November through February. Picnic tables overlook the mountains and lakes in several locations along the trail system. The Strider Kids Program helps local children to cross-country ski. In addition, for older folks, Tamarack runs a season-long Master's training program for skiers from beginner to expert. Mammoth Lakes is a bustling recreational community with numerous motels, restaurants, and stores.

Favorite Trails **Lake Mary Road** and **Lake Mary Loop** are the backbone of the trail system. First, you must wind up Twin Lakes Road to get to Lake Mary Road, which is literally a road up to the lake; in fact you can see the road signs along the side of the trail. You may wonder how someone skiing up this hill has to worry about a 25 mph speed limit, but wait until you are bombing back down! At an intersection with the Lake Mary Loop, turn right onto Lake Mary Road and you quickly reach a picnic table and lovely vista of Lake Mary. As the climb just about tops off, take a left onto the Lake Mary Loop and circle the lake on a fairly level trail, enjoying mountain and lake sights along the way. Lake Mary Road provides access to Mary, George, Mamie, and Horseshoe lakes. It is also an access road for backcountry skiers and snowshoers, who are allowed to travel on the side of the trail while venturing out to the surrounding wilderness. If you continue past the first entrance to the Lake Mary Loop you can access several other trails that lead up to the lakes. One of these is the Horseshoe Lake trail. Take Lake Mary Road to the second Lake Mary Loop junction, ski across the dam and turn right at the junction onto the **Horseshoe Lake** trail. This enjoyable loop flows up and down through a forest of lodgepole pines before opening up to a

The High Sierra backdrop at Mammoth

panoramic view of Horseshoe Lake and the high peaks to the west. You now travel along the lakeshore, past the CO_2 warning area, and onto the Falls Tract Trail. This short, delightful trail loops back around to Lake Mary Road. From its intersection with Falls Tract, Lake Mary Road is quite level and loops past Lake Mamie to its intersection with the Lake Mary Loop.

The **Lake George Loop** is a short figure-eight trail accessed off the Horseshoe trail near Lake Mary, or via the short, steep Voodoo trail. It provides views of Lake George.

Coldwater Loop–Mineshaft–Pine City–Lucky Strike–Waarlis Wrath–Bobby's Blast is a fun series of trails that furnish a way back from Lake Mary and are

 A Note about CO₂

An area just north of Horseshoe Lake has been designated as a CO_2 hazardous area. Higher than normal amounts of carbon dioxide have vented from the ground, killing trees. It is believed that earthquake activity in 1989 disturbed the ground and provided channels for the toxic gas to reach the surface. Carbon dioxide is heavier then air, and gas levels can build up in the snowpack. The Forest Service recommends staying out of the designated CO_2 area, which is just north of Horseshoe Lake. Skiers should be safe as none of the resort's trails go through the designated zone, but if you do decide to ski off track, the CO_2 area would not be the place to do it.

the highlight of the Mammoth Marathon ski race. From the Lake Mary Loop, the trail leads uphill on Coldwater Loop. The steady uphill tops out at the Mineshaft. Now you are starting a series of five trails that head more or less straight back to the lodge. The trails are narrow and a delight, with lots of shorts ups and downs through thick forest. Some drops are moderately steep, but quickly followed by level or uphill sections, so most skiers will feel comfortable. Mineshaft becomes a little easier as it turns into Pine City, and then gets slightly steeper again as Lucky Strike, which crosses Lake Mary Road. Here you can ski down the more gentle Lake Mary Road, or continue across to Waarlis Wrath, a narrow trail winding down the ridge, which blasts into Bobby's Blast. This trail then quickly drops down to the lodge.

Several short easy loops are also available at Tamarack. **Twin Lakes Loop** crosses a bridge between two lakes, then follows a short circle back to the start. **Vista** and **Dome** are two interconnected easy trails that narrowly wind through a thick forest. They provide a mountain vista to the southwest, and then a view of the Mammoth Mountain downhill ski area to the northeast.

Events and Races Mammoth is host to several good races including: the Tannenbaum 10-km Classic, in December; Lakes Basin 15-km Skate Race, in January; and the Allan Bard 20-km Classic, in February. At the end of March or in early April its time for the Mammoth Marathon, a wonderful event and one of the largest races in the Sierra. Racers can test their abilities against the 42-km course (the length of a runner's marathon), or go for the half-marathon instead. If the temperatures are not too warm the course will not be overly difficult, and you get to experience the best of Tamarack Cross-Country along the way. Once when I did the race the toughest part was the 50-mph winds across Horseshoe Lake. If it is warm and the snow conditions are slushy, however, be prepared for an arduous day. There is a wonderful après race party with plenty of good food and laughter. For strong cross-country skiers the Mammoth Marathon is an excellent way to end the ski season.

Mammoth Lakes Nordic Trail System

While in Mammoth you can also try the Mammoth Lakes Nordic Trail System. A few kilometers of nordic trails right in the center of town are groomed and maintained by the town of Mammoth Lakes and the Mammoth Nordic Club, a nonprofit organization. These trails are available to the public for free. For more information go to www.mammothnordic.com.

Gee, perhaps this photo was staged?
(Photo courtesy of Montecito-Sequoia Cross-Country Ski Resort)

Summer Bonuses Mammoth Lakes and the eastern Sierra are spectacular summertime outdoor playgrounds. The hiking and mountain biking is world class and both the Ansel Adams and John Muir Wilderness Areas are just a few miles away. Tioga Pass into Yosemite is about 45 minutes away, and the North and South Lake Trailheads, providing access to the John Muir Trail, are about an hour away, outside of Bishop.

Lodging and Restaurants Tamarack Lodge is right on the grounds of the nordic ski area. It is truly a unique experience to spend a few days at a lodge, ski every day, and never get in your car. But if you want to get in the car, the town of Mammoth Lakes is just a few miles away and is packed full of restaurants, stores, bars, and anything else you can think of that is usually in a big ski town.

Kids learn to ski at Montecito-Sequoia. (Photo courtesy of Montecito-Sequoia Cross-Country Ski Resort)

Montecito-Sequoia Cross-Country Ski Resort

Closest Town Fresno, CA, 75 miles

Directions From northern California take CA 99 south to CA 180 in Fresno. Take 180 to Chestnut Street, which you follow until it becomes CA 180 again. From here it is 65 miles to the Kings Canyon National Park entrance station. Continue 1.5 miles to the Y, turn right on Generals Highway, and go 8 miles south to the Montecito-Sequoia sign; look for three bears at the entrance. Turn right and take the half-mile long driveway to the lodge.

Note Be sure to gas up in Fresno; there are no gas stations in the park or in the surrounding area. During heavy snow periods an escort service is provided to guide your car into the resort. Be sure to call ahead to check on weather and road conditions.

Elevations 7,500 to 8,400 feet

Kilometers of Trails Up to 80 km (not every trail is groomed every day, and some are groomed only occasionally)

Contact 8000 Generals Highway, Kings Canyon National Park, CA 93633; 559-565-3388 or 1-800-843-8677; www.mslodge.com

Montecito-Sequoia is a unique and wonderful place. After a long and lonely drive from Fresno, you arrive at the snow-covered lodge surrounded by rustic cabins, and will really feel like you are in the middle of nowhere. The lodge is set up as an all-inclusive enclave, where once you are checked in you never have to get back in the car again, and skiing is available right out the door of your cabin. The views of the surrounding mountains are spectacular and a variety of interesting trails are available. The food is served buffet style and should satisfy most peoples needs, and the big old funky lodge with fireplaces and comfy couches is an excellent spot to relax and absorb the day. If it is clear, the large deck bakes in the sunshine and opens up to views of dozens of high Sierra peaks to the east. In addition to nordic skiing, Montecito-Sequoia has a small lift for beginning snowboarding and tubing, and a program of winter activities for kids.

Special Features The most special feature is that

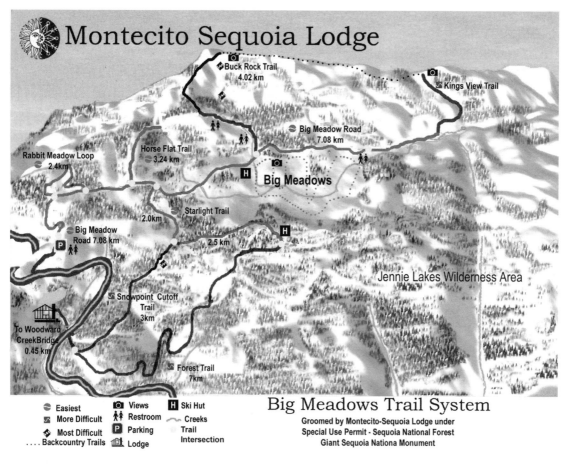

Montecito Sequoia Lodge

Buck Rock Trail
4.02 km

Kings View Trail

Big Meadow Road
7.08 km

Rabbit Meadow Loop
2.4km

Horse Flat Trail
3.24 km

H Big Meadows

Big Meadow
Road 7.08 km

Starlight Trail

2.0 km

2.5 km

H

Jennie Lakes Wilderness Area

Snowpoint Cutoff
Trail
3km

To Woodward
CreekBridge
0.45 km

Forest Trail
7km

🍃 Easiest	📷 Views	H Ski Hut	
🎿 More Difficult	🚻 Restroom	〰 Creeks	
◆ Most Difficult	P Parking	⬡ Trail Intersection	
.... Backcountry Trails	🏛 Lodge		

Big Meadows Trail System

Groomed by Montecito-Sequoia Lodge under
Special Use Permit - Sequoia National Forest
Giant Sequoia Nationa Monument

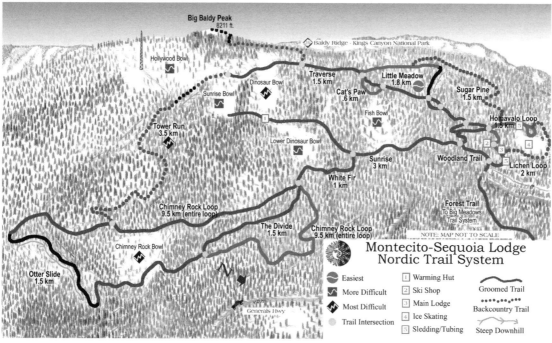

Big Baldy Peak
8211 ft.

Baldy Ridge · Kings Canyon National Park

Hollywood Bowl

Traverse
1.5 km

Little Meadow
1.8 km

Sugar Pine
1.5 km

Dinosaur Bowl

Sunrise Bowl

Cat's Paw
.6 km

Homavalo Loop
1.5 km

Tower Run
3.5 km

Fish Bowl

Lower Dinosaur Bowl

Woodland Trail

Lichen Loop
2 km

Sunrise
3 km

White Fir
1 km

Chimney Rock Loop
9.5 km (entire loop)

The Divide
1.5 km

Chimney Rock Loop
9.5 km (entire loop)

Forest Trail
To Big Meadows
Trail System

NOTE: MAP NOT TO SCALE

Chimney Rock Bowl

Otter Slide
1.5 km

Generals Hwy

Montecito-Sequoia Lodge
Nordic Trail System

🍃 Easiest	1 Warming Hut	〜 Groomed Trail
🎿 More Difficult	2 Ski Shop	
◆ Most Difficult	3 Main Lodge	•••• Backcountry Trail
⬡ Trail Intersection	4 Ice Skating	
	5 Sledding/Tubing	〜 Steep Downhill

Maps © Montecito-Sequoia Cross-Country Ski Resort

you can come for several days, leave your car in the parking lot, and everything is taken care of for you. There is a yurt with great views at the top of the Sunrise trail, and a hut near the Big Meadow. If you want to try something other then groomed cross-country skiing they also have tubing, snowboarding, and sledding, as well as backcountry skiing in several small bowls accessible via the nordic trails. Breakfast, lunch, and dinner are served right at the resort and are included in the price (which is a good thing since there are no other restaurants nearby). Walk out your cabin door, put your skis on, and go.

A 15-minute drive from the lodge will take you to the General Grant Grove of sequoias. A walking trail leads through the grove, and if you have not seen a big sequoia before you are in for an awesome experience. These huge trees are a deep, rusty orange and each seems to have its own personality and character. In comparison with their cousins, the redwoods, sequoias are much wider, but not as tall. The groves here are less dense than most Sierra forests, the trunks spread out enough that you can really see the whole tree standing alone in the sunshine. If you go to Montecito, a side trip to the grove is highly recommended.

Favorite Trails The **Sunrise** trail to the yurt is a pleasant out-and-back trip with plenty of ups and downs, spectacular views, and a yurt to escape the elements. Start on a rolling downhill with several switchbacks to a junction, then an open sunny uphill brings you to the yurt.

Take the 15-km **Chimney Rock Loop**—route of the former Chimney Rock Challenge—and enjoy the best of the Montecito trail system. The route follows Sunrise downhill to a junction where you take White Fir downhill some more to the Chimney Rock Loop on your right. This gentle uphill through the trees is followed by the steep downhill of the Otter Slide, before heading steadily uphill back to the lodge. It can be skied either direction and is fun and challenging whichever way you choose. Up until a few years ago the Chimney Rock Challenge was a regular race on the circuit; many hope it will be placed back on the calender some day.

Begin climbing **Little Meadow** right up from the lodge along a ridge to the short Cat's Paw loop, which provides mountain vistas in two directions. If groomed past here, you can continue all the way to Baldy Ridge and Peak via the Traverse trail.

About a mile from the lodge is a second trailhead for the **Big Meadow trails,** which are open to the general public and used by snowmobilers as well as skiers. The beginner Big Meadow trail heads up on a wide road past Rabbit Run (a really nice loop that tends to get less snowmobile use) to the wide-open Big Meadow. If you time it right, in springtime or after a period of warm days and cold nights, this meadow can be perfect for skating. I still smile when I think about the warm January day that we spent skiing around and around this meadow when the skating conditions were perfect. Several trails lead steeply uphill off the Big Meadow trail to the ridge above where you will find panoramic views of the meadow and surrounding mountains.

Summer Bonuses Montecito-Sequoia is a summer lodge as well as winter resort. Located right in the heart of the Sierra you can enjoy the nearby hiking in Kings Canyon National Park, the sequoia grove, or just kick back and relax in the trees.

Lodging and Restaurants You are at the lodging and restaurants. It is all here, which is good, because there is nothing between here and Fresno. Hope you like it.

Five Reasons to Go to Montecito-Sequoia

1. You don't have to worry about a thing. Every aspect of your stay is taken care of. Walk out the door and ski; when you are hungry, walk into the lodge to eat.
2. The scenery is truly inspiring and the trails lead from one beautiful vista to another.
3. It is a great place for a family to come with the kids, kick back, and relax.
4. The spectacular sequoia grove nearby.
5. You will feel like you are going back in time.

Quick Pick

Yosemite Mountaineering and Cross-Country Ski Center at Badger Pass (Glacier Point Road)

Closest Towns Yosemite Valley, 20 miles; Oakhurst, 39 miles; Fresno, 84 miles

It might be hard to drag yourself away from this view to go skiing.

Half Dome and Nevada Falls from Glacier Point Road

Directions In winter you can access Badger Pass via three routes:

1. CA 120: From Groveland drive about 42 miles east to the park entrance at Big Oak Flat. Continue toward Yosemite Valley 10 miles, then take CA 41 for 10 miles to Glacier Point Road, which you follow 5 miles to Badger Pass.
2. CA 140: From Mariposa, CA 140 enters the park at the Arch Rock Entrance, continue into the valley and take CA 41 as above.
3. CA 41: From Fresno drive through Oakhurst, then drive an additional 34 miles to the Glacier Point Rd, which you take 5 miles to Badger Pass.

From late fall through the winter and spring the east entrance into Yosemite National Park at Tioga Pass is closed.

Contact P.O. Box 578, Yosemite National Park, CA 95389; 209-372-8444; www.badgerpass.com

The cross-country skiing facility at Badger Pass, which is located just across the parking lot from the downhill resort, provides a 17-km groomed trail out to

Racers try not to turn around and stare at Half Dome in the Glacier Point Race.

Glacier Point. The trail is wide, well groomed, and follows the course of the unplowed Glacier Point Road to spectacular views of Half Dome and Yosemite Valley. The area also has a quick, steep, 3-km trail. In addition to the groomed trails, there are over 90 miles of marked trails for backcountry skiers, most of which depart from Glacier Point Rd. While there is a fee to enter Yosemite National Park, there is no additional charge to use the cross-country ski trails at Glacier Point.

The Glacier Point hut is located at the end of the Glacier Point trail. It overlooks Yosemite Valley and Half Dome at one of the most awesome viewpoints you will find anywhere. And perhaps the best part is that unlike in the summer months, in the winter there are no tour buses, no hordes of tourists to detract from the experi-

ence. The Glacier Point hut is designed to accommodate up to 20 skiers in dorm-style lodging. It is a rustic and charming lodge that is wood-heated. Perhaps the best way to experience Yosemite Cross-Country is to go to the Nordic Holiday Races in late February. There is a 15-km striding race on Saturday and a 34-km skating race on Sunday out to Glacier Point and back. The Glacier Point race course is well groomed, and while it is certainly not flat, is not especially difficult.

Yosemite Valley is just 30 minutes away from Badger Pass, and winter or spring are great times to see the valley. The crowds are much smaller and the waterfalls are roaring. Come to Yosemite in spring and spend the morning cross-country skiing and the afternoon enjoying the valley's beauty.

Tim's Top 10 Tips for Skiing at Cross-Country Ski Centers

1. ***Ski early in the morning, especially in springtime.*** If it has been a week or more since it snowed, the days sunny and warm, and the nights cold and clear, it is especially important to ski in the morning. The colder the nights, the later in the morning you should ski. If the days are warm and the nights not very cold, then you need to ski as soon as the resort opens in the morning, the earlier the better. When it is snowing the day you are skiing, it is less important to ski first thing in the morning. In fact it is best to wait until the grooming machines have had time to catch up to the snow. If it is really snowing hard, you want to follow about fifteen minutes behind the grooming machine so you are skiing on freshly groomed snow.

2. ***Skating is best on firm, older snow.*** Usually a few days after the most recent storm. Striding is good on brand new, cold snow. If you also like to downhill ski, ski downhill the first day after a big storm, stride the second day, and skate the third day. If you are a skating addict like me, stride the first day and then skate the next two days.

3. ***Follow the season when picking the nordic area and the trails you'd like to ski.*** Royal Gorge is a great early season choice, because they get a lot of snow in fall. Spooner is good for long midwinter loops, as is Tahoe Donner. Is it a windy and snowy day? Try Tahoe Cross-Country or Bear Valley, where sheltered trails provide a break from the elements. Late season? Even though they get less snow than several other areas, Tahoe Cross-Country often has the longest season because they groom it until they can't.

4. ***Take a lesson.*** If you are new to cross-country skiing, especially if you are new to skate skiing, a lesson can make a world of difference. Just figuring out the basics, from body position to poling techniques, can turn a grueling workout into a heck of a fun ski (although perhaps still a grueling workout).

5. ***Wax your skis regularly.*** The bottoms of your skis should be black and smooth. If the bottoms of your skis are starting to take on the hue of snow, it is definitely long past time to wax. While racers and skiers with lots of time

on their hands wax every time they ski, most people can can wax every second or third time and still find their skis fast enough. (For waxing how-tos see pages 18–20.)

6. **Ski regularly, enjoy life.** The key to learning how to cross-country ski is to put time on your skis. In the ski lesson business we talk about striding being easy to learn and hard to master, while skating is hard to learn and easy to master. Both techniques have one thing in common: The more you ski, the better you will ski. Don't give up if you feel like you are not an expert after one lesson. A lesson teaches you what to do, and then you have to go out and ski to really learn how to do it. Also the more you ski, the stronger your ski muscles become, which makes skiing easier and more fun. So go ski.

7. **Stay flexible.** Add a yoga practice or stretching program to your ski training. While skiing will strengthen your muscles and aerobic capacity, you need to stretch to remain flexible and prevent injury. I recommend yoga a few times a week. It not only aids flexibility but it is relaxing and fun. (To find a yoga studio in Sierra mountain communities, see page 84.)

8. **Ski with strong skiers.** Nothing will improve your skiing more than skiing with those who are a little stronger than you are. Having to ski a little faster and a little longer than you are comfortable with will make you a better skier. While it might hurt a bit, you can handle it because you are a cross-country skier, among the most athletically fit people in the world.

9. **Use top-of-the-line ski equipment.** Once you have decided that cross-country skiing is a sport for you, invest in good equipment; it makes a huge difference. Go for the best in skis, poles, and boots.

10. **Stop and enjoy the view.** Sure you should ski hard and get in shape, but stop to smell the trees (Jeffrey pines smell like butterscotch) and revel in the beauty of the mountains. Bring your friends and have a picnic. Enjoy the quiet and the mountains and smile—you are in the right place.

Best Ski Areas to . . .

See Beautiful Views

Views are subjective and every nordic center has wonderful views, but my favorites are:

- The Sierra Vista and Last Round Up trails at Kirkwood are perhaps the prettiest trails I have seen. They give you a real feeling of being in the wilderness.
- The Silver Trail at Tahoe Cross-Country has great views of Lake Tahoe and Mt. Rose from a sunny slope.
- From Point Mariah at Royal Gorge you can look west down into the Royal Gorge, 4,000 feet down to the American River. To the east, view the Sierra crest, from Mt. Lincoln to Mt. Anderson and beyond.
- Saint's Rest at Spooner Lake offers stunning vistas of Lake Tahoe. If you are familiar with the world-famous Flume Trail, the views are similar.
- Euer Valley at Tahoe Donner is a beautiful ski in a wide-open mountain valley, with views of Castle Peak and the Frog Lake Cliffs.

- Spend a few minutes staring at Half Dome from Glacier Point in Yosemite, then wipe that drool off your face.

Ski Alone (or at Least Close to Alone)

First off, ski early in the morning and midweek. Then, ski at these locations:

- Ski the Schneider trail system at Kirkwood and perhaps you will have the place to yourself. Remember this rule: The farther up the hill you go, the fewer people you will see.
- At Spooner Lake, take the long, steep road up to Marlette Lake and leave the small crowd at the beginner trails farther down.
- To get to the quiet, you have to go through the noise of the village at Northstar and downhill area, but once you get to the nordic trails, it will be quiet.

Get Good Grub

- Tahoe Donner serves up healthy meals and soups. You can always count on Tahoe Donner to provide great healthy food.
- The food at the Royal Gorge lodge is fairly basic, but if you take the Rainbow Interconnect trail, or spend the night at the Rainbow Lodge, you are in for some fine gourmet dining at the Engadine Café. In addition, The Ice Lakes Lodge and restaurant is right across from the trails at Serene Lakes.
- The Lakeview Restaurant at Tamarack Lodge is one of the more popular restaurants in the Mammoth Lakes area.
- Tahoe Cross-Country has just added a new café in the lodge. It provides excellent soups, sandwiches, salads, and espresso drinks.
- The on-trail café at Bear Valley serves up good fare, and with a great view to boot.

Buy a Season Pass

- Nothing else even comes close: When you buy a season pass at Tahoe Cross-Country you get a card for free cookies and coffee throughout the season. Then there is the kilometer club. Keep track of your skiing distances throughout the season, and when you surpass kilometer-stones like 500 and 1000, you win prizes, including clothing, books, and gift certificates. Finally, Tahoe Cross-Country's rolling terrain makes it the perfect place to ski day after day and still be able to walk at night.

Ski All Day Long

- The Rainbow Interconnect at Royal Gorge is only open some weekends at the highest snow periods of the year, and if it is open be sure to take advantage of this treat. Starting out at the Royal Gorge lodge you travel mostly downhill, sometimes steeply, all the way to the Rainbow Lodge. From there have a drink and some food, and then catch the shuttle back to the main lodge. Even if the Interconnect is closed,

there are several long skis at Royal Gorge that will do the job of wearing you out. Ski out to Devil's Peak or Point Mariah and you will be pleasantly spent by the time you return.
- Try the 40-km Carson Range trail at Spooner Lake for a long day of spectacular views, incredible skiing, and a heck of a lot of climbing and descending. At the end you will be so exhausted all you will be able to do is relax in a recliner, but you will have a smile on your face.

Ski the Biggest Grunt

Looking for a long, difficult climb? Try one of these:
- At Tahoe Donner, ski from the lodge to the top of Drifter via Crazy Horse. If you want to make it even harder (actually, much harder), ski down into Euer Valley first and then start heading uphill on I'M O.K., Euer O.K. I'm getting tired just thinking about it.
- At Royal Gorge, ski out to Point Mariah. Then take Sterlings Canyon up to Razorback. A big climb with a big reward at the top.
- Ski from the Spooner Lake lodge to the top of the Marlette Saddle and on to the Carson Range Trail. This is a long one, but the views are worth it. Don't miss the Super G downhill on the way back.
- Begin on Kirkwood's Outpost Trail at the Schneider Trailhead. Go up, up, up to Sierra Vista. Then take a deep breath and enjoy the vista.
- Try the Billy Dutton Uphill Race. It only comes 'round once a year, but it is one heck of a steep uphill. Once you get to the top have a party and jump in the hot tub.

Ski Out the Door

- Montecito-Sequoia: Spend the weekend with a nice cozy group. Food is included, and you really can ski out the back door of your cabin (which is also your front door).
- Spooner Lake Log Cabins: Two charming, secluded log cabins available to rent right next to the trails. Does it get any better than that?

- Rainbow Lodge and Ice Lakes Lodge, Royal Gorge: At the Rainbow Lodge, you can't ski out your back door, but you can take the shuttle to the base lodge, and if the Rainbow Interconnect is open, you can ski home to your back door. And breakfast and dinner at the Engadiné Cafe are magnificent. At Ice Lakes Lodge, you can enjoy wonderful lodging, then walk across the quiet street to the trails.
- Mammoth's Tamarack Lodge is right on the trail system and has an excellent restaurant as well.
- Bear Valley: It's just a short walk from the lodging at Basecamp or Bear Valley Lodge to Bear Valley's cross-country trails.

Find a Ghost

- Royal Gorge's Rainbow Lodge. This old rustic lodge is said to harbor a friendly female ghost. I have stayed there several times and never encountered her, but perhaps the hot chocolate and peppermint schnapps by the fire made me immune to her charms.

Take Your Dog

- Tahoe Cross-Country allows dogs on 8 km all day midweek and in the afternoons on weekends. The dog trails are very popular, and you can even get a doggy season pass.
- Kirkwood allows dogs on two trails, including the popular High Trail.

Look at the Trees

- Tahoe Cross-Country: Situated right at the transition elevation between several different tree ecosystems, this area allows you to see a variety of beautiful mountain trees. Close to the lodge are a few huge incense cedars, as well as sugar pines, white firs, and Jeffrey pines. As you go up in altitude you move into red firs, western white pines, and hemlocks.
- Montecito-Sequoia: While the area around the

lodge has some nice firs and pines, if you take the 15-minute drive to the General's Grove, you can wander through a spectacular grove of giant sequoias.
- Kirkwood: While lodgepole pines are the dominant trees at Kirkwood, the real beauties are the numerous craggy junipers that cling to life among the boulders. They look like giant bundles of broccoli and are truly exquisite.
- Bear Valley: Here you will also see some great juniper specimens, but the highlights are the groves of huge aspen trees.

Ski Early or Late in the Season

- Royal Gorge, especially at the Van Norden Trail system, where it stays really cold and keeps the snow in good shape in fall or spring when other areas have melted out. In fall it is especially nice to ease into shape by making your first ski on the level Van Norden terrain.
- Kirkwood is at a higher elevation than other Sierra ski areas and receives more snow than almost anywhere else in the United States. It is especially a nice place to enjoy some great spring skiing. It doesn't get much better than spending a sunny spring morning on the Schneider Camp trails with awesome views of Round Top Mountain.
- Tahoe Cross-Country is not in the deepest snow area, but it does makes a concerted effort to keep the large base of season pass holders happy by staying open as long as possible. In some years they stay open several weeks later than other ski areas in the Lake Tahoe region.

Ski in a Spring Meadow

In the spring, or sometimes in the middle of the winter if the conditions are right (several weeks of warm days and cold nights), the snow sets up nice and firm on the flat meadows, allowing skate skiing off-trail. If you find these conditions, go for it; you are in for some great skiing. But don't dilly-dally, because spring conditions don't last long.

- Antone Meadows at Tahoe Cross-Country: Ski the Orange or Red trail to the large meadow and Burton Creek.
- Big Meadow at Montecito-Sequoia: Take the Big Meadow trail to Big Meadow, and then ski all around the big meadow.
- The Euer Valley at Tahoe Donner: Go to Euer Valley via the Last Round-up trail. The best skating is on the north side of the loop.
- At Spooner Lake, skate the meadow areas close to the lodge. Ski to the North Canyon trail about 1 km to the meadows on your left.
- The Horseshoe Hut area at Royal Gorge, just off the Stage Coach and Wagon Train trails.
- Kirkwood's Last Round-up circles through a big open bowl that has lots of open space for skating or telemarking.

Enjoy an Event or Race

Just about every cross-country area has a signature event that is worth attending. Here are a few of interest:

- The Great Ski Race at Tahoe Cross-Country. The 30-km route from Tahoe City to Truckee is the focus of a popular point-to-point race that often attracts over 1,000 participants. Tahoe Cross-Country also presents The Gourmet Ski Tour in March. It's more about eating than skiing, but who's complaining?
- The 20-km Bjornloppet at Bear Valley has been a popular race for many years and a good excuse to venture there.
- The Echo to Kirkwood Race ends at the Kirkwood nordic center after a lot of climbing and descending, much of it off-trail.
- Yosemite's Glacier Point Skate Race: You may have driven out to Glacier Point; doesn't it sound better to ski out to it? It is a long way—34 km out and back—but the terrain is not too difficult. Don't forget to stop and enjoy the view.
- Royal Gorge combines the Gold Rush, 50 km, Silver Rush, 25 km, and the Bronze Rush, 15 km, into a big race event that attracts top talent from around the country.

- The 42-km Mammoth Marathon occurs in the spring and is a fun and challenging personal test.
- The Billy Dutton Uphill isn't connected to any nordic ski area, and in fact is located on a downhill ski run at Squaw Valley USA. Only 5 km—how hard can it be? Really hard, because you climb 2,000 feet from the bottom of Squaw Valley to the top of the tram.
- The Ernie Woodfill Memorial Race at Mt. Shasta is half off-trail and half on. Most people ski the first leg with skating skis, then switch to striding skis for the backcountry portion. An interesting race with lots of character and personality, and some pretty fun prizes.

Unfortunately, cross-country ski races come and go on a regular basis. Visit www.farwestnordic.org for detailed information on which races and events are happening in the Sierra this year.

Ski on a Snowy Day

- Since most of Tahoe Cross-Country's trails wind through the shelter of the forest, it is a pleasurable ski even in a big snowstorm. I have skied there several times when the trails were freshly groomed while nearby areas were closed.
- Many of Bear Valley's trails are shielded from the wind, and when you finish skiing the restaurants and bars are just a short walk away.

Relax in a Lodge

- Auburn Ski Club's 6,000-square-foot lodge is light, airy, and a pleasure to hang out in. If there happens to be a high school ski race right out the door, then step onto the huge sun deck and enjoy the view.
- Montecito-Sequoia's large lodge is very relaxing and a great place to kick back. Which is a good thing, because as a destination resort, you will be doing a lot of kicking back at Montecito.
- Bear Valley's quiet little on-trail café is a

friendly place to have a meal and watch skiers slide by.

- During the week at Tahoe Cross-Country you can lie on the couch next to the woodstove, use the wi-fi on your laptop, or perhaps nod off for a few moments (just don't tell the boss).
- At Royal Gorge enjoy the fire and snuggler at Rainbow Lodge or Ice Lakes Lodge.

Tim's Top 10 Trails

H ere it is, for your entertainment. Drum roll, please. My recommendations for the top 10 cross-country ski trails in the Sierra, in no particular order, are the following:

- Drifter, Tahoe Donner

- Super G, Spooner Lake

- Silver, Tahoe Cross-Country

- Last Round Up, Kirkwood

- Last Round-Up, Tahoe Donner

- Bronze, Tahoe Cross-Country

- Devil's Peak, Royal Gorge

- Horseshoe Lake Loop, Mammoth Lakes

- Marlette Lake Trail, Spooner Lake

- Point Mariah, Royal Gorge

Resources and Information

Ski Areas

Auburn Ski Club
P.O. Box 829
Soda Springs, CA 95728
530-426-3313
www.auburnskiclub.org

Bear Valley Cross Country and Adventure Company
1 Bear Valley Road
P.O. Box 5120
Bear Valley, CA 95223
209-753-2834
www.bearvalleyxc.com

Kirkwood Cross-Country Ski Area
c/o Kirkwood Mountain Resort
P.O. Box 1
Kirkwood, CA 95646
Cross-Country Center: 209-258-7248
Kirkwood Lodging Services: 1-800-967-7500
Ski Report Hotline: 1-877-Kirkwood
www.kirkwood.com

Montecito-Sequoia Cross Country Resort
8000 Generals Highway

Kings Canyon National Park, CA 93633
559-565-3388; 1-800-843-8677
www.mslodge.com

Mt. Shasta Nordic Center
P.O. Box 765
Mt. Shasta, CA 96067
530-926-2142
www.mtshastanordic.org

Northstar-at-Tahoe™ Resort Cross-Country Ski & Snowshoe Center
11025 Pioneer Trail, Suite G100
Truckee, CA 96161
530-562-2475; 1-800-Go North
www.northstarattahoe.com

Royal Gorge
P.O. Box 1100
Soda Springs, CA 95728
530-426-3871
www.royalgorge.com

Spooner Lake Cross-Country
P.O. Box 981
Carson City, NV 89702
775-749-5349; 1-888-858-8844
www.spoonerlake.com; www.theflumetrail.com

Squaw Creek Nordic Center
400 Squaw Creek Road
P.O. Box 3333
Olympic Valley, CA 96146
530-583-6300 ext. 5507
www.squawcreek.com

Tahoe Cross-Country Ski Area
P.O. Box 7260
Tahoe City, CA 96145
530-583-5475
www.tahoexc.org

Tahoe Donner Cross-Country
15275 Alder Creek Road
Truckee, CA 96161
530-587-9484
www.tdxc.com

Tamarack Cross-Country Ski Center at Mammoth Mountain
P.O. Box 69
Mammoth Lakes, CA 93456
760-934-2442; 1-800 Mammoth
www.mammothmountain.com

Yosemite Mountaineering and Cross-Country Ski Center at Badger Pass
P.O. Box 578
Yosemite National Park, CA 95389
209-372-8444
www.badgerpass.com

Books

White, Michael C. *Snowshoe Trails of Tahoe*. Berkeley, CA: Wilderness Press, 1998.

Libkind, Marcus. *Lake Tahoe*. Vol. 1 of *Ski Tours in the Sierra Nevada*. 2nd ed. Livermore, CA: Bittersweet Publishing, 1995.

Hindman, Steve. *Cross-Country Skiing: Building Skills for Fun and Fitness*. Seattle: Mountaineers Books, 2005.

Cazeneuve, Brian and Jules Older. *Cross-Country Skiing: A Complete Guide*. New York: W.W. Norton, 1995.

Peterson, Paul, Rick Lovett, and John Morton. *The Essential Cross-Country Skier*. New York: McGraw-Hill, 1999.

Brown, Nat, and Natalie Brown-Gutnik. *The Complete Guide to Cross-Country Ski Preparation*. Seattle: Mountaineers Books, 1999.

Gaskill, Steven E. *Fitness Cross-Country Skiing*. Champion, IL: Human Kinetics Publishers, 1998.

Meloche, Lisa, and David McMahon. *Tao of Skiing: Aide Memoire for Cross-Country Skiing Aficionados*. Cold Fusion Heavy Industries, 1999.

Svensson, Einer. *Ski Skating with Champions: How to Ski with Less Energy*. Seattle: Ski Skating with Champions, 1995.

Weisel, Jonathan. *Cross-Country Ski Vacations: A Guide to the Best Resorts, Lodges, and Groomed Trails in North America*. Emeryville, CA: Avalon Travel Publishing, 1999.

Magazines

Cross-Country Skier
P.O. Box 550
Cable, WI 54821
1-800-827-0607
www.crosscountryskier.com

The Master Skier
P.O. Box 187
Escanaba, MI 49829
906-789-1139
www.masterskier.com

The *Master Skier* is a great publication with tips on skiing and racing. Pick up a copy at your local nordic center and check out their Web site.

Ski Trax
317 Adelaide Street, W. Suite 703
Toronto, ON Canada M5V 1P9
416-977-2100
www.skitrak.com

Organizations

Far West Nordic
P.O. Box 10015
Truckee, CA 96162
530-587-0304
www.farwestnordic.org

The regional nordic organization for cross-country skiing and racing. The best place to get the latest on races and race results.

American Cross-Country Skiers
P.O. Box 604
Bend, OR 97709
www.xcskiworld.com

An awesome Web site with tons of information and ski tips.

Cross-Country Ski Areas Association
603-239-4341
www.xcski.org

The association and Web site for owners and managers of North America's cross-country ski areas, it also has plenty of information for us plain folks.

Ski Equipment Manufacturers

Alpina: www.alpinasports.com

Atomic Ski USA: www.atomicsnow.com

Fischer Sports USA: www.us.fischer-ski.com

Karhu: www.karhu.com

Madshus: www.madshus.com

Rossignol Skis Inc.: www.rossignol.com

Solda Wax: www.soldaskiwax.com

SolomonSports: www.salomonsports.com

Swix Sports: www.swixsport.com or www.swixschool.no

Toko Wax: www.tokous.com/NordicMain.htm and www.tokous.com/racewaxtips.htm

Yoko Poles: www.yokopoles.com

Yoga Studios

While in a ski town, spend a morning or evening in a yoga class. It is relaxing and will help you stay limber to ski stronger and avoid injury. Here are a few studios that might meet your needs:

Kings Beach
Lake Tahoe Wellness Center
695 Wolf Street
Kings Beach, CA 96143
530-546-8201
www.laketahoewellnesscenter.com

Mammoth Lakes
Tadasan Yoga
3059 Chateau Road
Mammoth Lakes, CA 93546
760-924-8746
www.tadasanyoga.com

Mt. Shasta
Shasta Yoga Center
201 North Mt. Shasta Boulevard
Mt. Shasta City, CA 96067
530-926-0221
www.amycooperyoga.com

South Lake Tahoe
Mountain Yoga
585 Tahoe Keys Boulevard
South Lake Tahoe, CA 96150
530-543-1400
www.mountain-yoga.com

Tahoe City
The Yoga Space, Tahoe
Cobblestone Shopping Center
475 North Lake Boulevard
Tahoe City, CA 96145
530-581-1933
www.yogaspacetahoe.com

Bikram Yoga Tahoe
The Boatworks Mall
760 North Lake Boulevard
Tahoe City, CA 96145
530-581-1841
www.bikramyogatahoe.com

Truckee
Tahoe Yoga and Wellness Center
10770 Donner Pass Road
Truckee, CA 96161
530-550-8333
www.tahoeyoga.com

Acknowledgments

Once again it was Sara Holm to the rescue. For the third straight book Sara read through the manuscript and came up with all sorts of great ideas and suggestions. A kindergarten teacher, Sara's perfectly trained for dealing with my writing.

The cross-country ski centers profiled in the book were all very helpful and encouraging. If you want to know why cross-country skiing is great, it is because of the down-to-earth, friendly attitude of the managers and owners of the resorts. Kevin Murnane at Tahoe Cross-Country was especially helpful, reading through the manuscript and offering suggestions. Karen Aldous of Mt. Shasta deserves special mention as she gave me the royal treatment when I visited her area and town. Bear Valley's Paul Peterson was also a font of great info and provided a good quote. Thanks to personal trainer Kathy Brown for her review of the section on training for a race. Thanks also to Royal Gorge, Auburn Ski Club, Tamarack at Mammoth Lakes, Northstar at Tahoe, Kirkwood, Montecito-Sequoia, Tahoe Donner, Spooner Lake, Resort at Squaw Creek, and Yosemite.

Kudos to the folks at The Countryman Press, including Jennifer Thompson and my editor Kristin Sperber. Of course I am full of all sorts of brilliant ideas, but they helped me make it sound really gooder.

A final thanks goes to all of my students over the years at Tahoe Cross-Country. I am sure they taught me more about skiing than I taught them. But I already knew the main lesson: Cross-country skiing is a lot of fun and should be done every day! Well, at least every day that there is enough snow.

A Final Note

Nordic centers have a tendency to come and go and make changes to their trail network and management on a regular basis. This is obviously a challenge to the writer and publisher to keep up to date. As I was finishing the manuscript for this book I e-mailed one ski area director who had been extremely helpful to me to let her know the book was being published. She e-mailed back, "Congratulations, but I no longer work there. You better check with the new management to see what changes they have planned." Such is life in the cross-country-ski world. I made every effort to get the most current information and apologize if some area has closed, a race no longer occurs, or trails have changed since publication.

One way to avoid closures is to support your local nordic center. They often operate on a shoestring and could always use your help. Go ski there, bring your friends, volunteer to help at a race, and by all means, eat and stay there. Please don't hesitate to e-mail suggestions for future editions or corrections at thauserman@ telis.org or contact the publisher at www.countryman press.com.